INSTRUCTIONS TO AUTHORS

I0797039

STATEMENT OF PURPOSE

The *Educational Psychologist* publishes scholarly essays, reviews, critiques, and articles of a theoretical/conceptual nature that contribute to our understanding of the issues, problems, and research associated with the field of educational psychology. Articles representing all aspects of educational psychology are encouraged. This journal, however, does not publish articles whose primary purpose is to report the method and results of an empirical study.

SUBMISSION OF MANUSCRIPTS

Manuscripts must be prepared in accordance with the following instructions.

FOLLOW APA STYLE

Authors should follow the *Publication Manual of the American Psychological Association* (4th ed.) in preparing manuscripts for submission to this journal. All manuscripts must be prefaced by an abstract of 100–150 words on a separate sheet. All manuscript pages, including reference lists and tables, must be typed double-spaced. All figures must be camera ready. Authors should comply with "Guidelines to Reduce Bias in Language" as printed in the *Publication Manual.* Manuscripts that fail to conform to APA-style guidelines will be returned to the author(s).

PREPARE FOR BLIND PEER REVIEW

All articles appearing in the *EP* are peer reviewed. Because the reviewers have agreed to participate in a blind reviewing system, authors submitting manuscripts are requested to include with each copy of the manuscript a cover sheet that shows the title of the manuscript, the names of the authors, the authors' institutional affiliations, the mailing address, the date the manuscript is submitted, and a running head. The first page of the manuscript should omit the authors' names and affiliations but should include the title of the manuscript and the date it is submitted. Footnotes containing information pertaining to the authors' identities or affiliations should be placed on separate pages. Every effort should be made by authors to see that the manuscript itself contains no clues to their identities.

SCREEN FOR APPROPRIATENESS

By submitting manuscripts to the *Educational Psychologist,* authors are confirming that the manuscripts have not been published and are not under consideration for publication elsewhere. Prior to submission, authors should determine whether their manuscripts correspond to the journal's statement of purpose—to publish essays, critiques, and articles of a theoretical/conceptual nature that contribute to our understanding of the issues, problems, and research associated with the field of educational psychology. Articles consistent with the journal's purpose include critical, integrative reviews of educational psychology research; conceptual or theoretical syntheses or analyses of educational psychology research; scientifically documented digests of educational psychology research relevant to policy issues; and documented, scholarly essays of general interest to the educational psychology community. Consistent with the journal's mission to serve as a forum for important ideas in educational psychology, articles of varying lengths and covering all aspects of educational psychology will be considered, including articles focusing on implications for educational theory, research, practice, or policy. Articles that report mainly the results of an empirical study (e.g., would be appropriate for the *Journal of Educational Psychology*) or articles that are intended mainly as practical guides (without research documentation) are inappropriate for the *EP* and will be returned to the authors. In addition to publishing regular articles, the journal publishes special issues that are devoted to important themes in educational psychology and keynote reviews with published peer commentary. Authors interested in the latter formats are requested to contact the editor prior to submitting a proposal for a special issue or keynote review.

FOLLOW COPYRIGHT LAWS

Authors are responsible for obtaining and providing written permission from copyright owners for reprinting previously published illustrations, tables, or lengthy quotes (500 or more words). Authors are responsible for the accuracy of the material in their manuscripts.

SUBMIT FOUR COPIES

Send five copies of your manuscripts (an original and four duplicates) to: Philip H. Winne and Lyn Corno, Coeditors, *Educational Psychologist,* Faculty of Education, Simon Fraser University, Burnaby, British Columbia, Canada V5A 1S6. Authors should keep a copy of the manuscript to guard against loss in the mail. After a manuscript is accepted for publication, its author is asked to provide a computer disk containing the manuscript file. Files are copyedited and typeset into page proofs. Authors read proofs to correct errors and answer editors' queries.

LETTERS TO THE EDITORS: Letters to the editors concerning published articles should be sent to the editors at the address listed under "Instructions to Authors."

SUBSCRIPTIONS AND CIRCULATION: The *Educational Psychologist* is mailed to all members of the Division of Educational Psychology (Division 15) of the American Psychological Association who are current in their divisional dues according to the official roster of names and addresses maintained at APA Headquarters in Washington, DC. Questions regarding the current status and address of Division 15 members should be addressed to the American Psychological Association, 750 First Street, NE, Washington, DC 20002–4242. Individuals who are not members of Division 15 may subscribe to the journal for $50 per volume (calendar year); library and institutional subscriptions are available for $330 per volume. Subscriptions outside the U.S.A. and Canada are: Individual $80; Institutional $360. Subscriptions for the 2001 volume are available on a calendar-year basis. Subscription requests for nonmembers should be addressed to Lawrence Erlbaum Associates, 10 Industrial Avenue, Mahwah, NJ 07430 2262.

BACK ISSUES: For information concerning back issues, write to Lawrence Erlbaum Associates at the above address. **CHANGE OF ADDRESS** (Division 15 membership): Contact Howard Everson, College Board, 45 Columbus Avenue, New York, NY 10023. **CHANGE OF ADDRESS** (nonmembers): Send notice of change of address to Subscription Department, Lawrence Erlbaum Associates, 10 Industrial Avenue, Mahwah, NJ 07430 2262 at least 30 days prior to the actual change of address. Claims for missing issues cannot be honored beyond 4 months after mailing date. Duplicate copies cannot be sent to replace issues not delivered due to failure to notify publisher of change of address.

First published 2001 by Lawrence Erlbaum Associates, Inc

Published 2019 by Routledge
2 Park Square, Milton Park, Abingdon, Oxon OX14 4RN
52 Vanderbilt Avenue, New York, NY 10017

Routledge is an imprint of the Taylor & Francis Group, an informa business

ISSN 0046 1520
ISBN 13: 978-0-8058-9706-7 (pbk)

Educational Psychologist

Official Publication of the
Division of Educational Psychology of the
American Psychological Association

Volume 36, Number 2, Spring 2001

EDUCATIONAL PSYCHOLOGIST, *36*(2), 69–72

Educational Psychology Yesterday, Today, and Tomorrow: Debate and Direction in an Evolving Field

Thomas L. Good and Joel R. Levin
Department of Educational Psychology
University of Arizona

The field of educational psychology is rich and diverse. Those who are not educational psychologists might be surprised by the increasingly diverse set of research topics that educational psychologists study empirically and theoretically. In fact, the scope of educational psychology is so rich that any educational psychologist can aspire to expertise knowledge in relatively few areas (see Berliner & Calfee, 1996). One reviewer (Wise, 1997) of the *Handbook of Educational Psychology* noted that the book was both hard to pick up (because of its size) and difficult to put down (because of the quality of the content). Despite the vastness of the field, it is ironic that some educators who are not integral scholars of educational psychology are able to write sweepingly and critically about a field in which they have but little knowledge (e.g., see Doyle & Carter, 1996).

This special issue is a follow up to a special issue that Phyllis Blumenfeld and Linda Anderson edited for the *Educational Psychologist* (1996). In part, it deals with the argument then presented that educational psychologists have little to offer to educational practice.[1] The primary purpose of this special issue is to respond to those who write pejoratively about the field of educational psychology. We do so by illustrating several ways in which the field has provided valuable theory and research to practitioners. In addition, we offer examples and arguments about how the field may profitably evolve in the future. Although only a small sample of work can be published here, it is hoped that this issue will touch off continuing discussion about where the field has been and where it is headed. It is important to note that this special issue was designed primarily with current and future students of educational psychology in mind. Fellow educational psychology professors and researchers are already well aware of controversies in the field.

EXPERT–NOVICE KNOWLEDGE

Sometimes noneducational psychologists who write on topics such as learning theory, the informal curriculum, motivation, and assessment are those who do not conduct research on the topics about which they write. Such wide "translation activity" is generally an unproductive avocation in most other academic fields. For example, university medical researchers who specialize in heart research tend not to write outside their area of specialization (i.e., as a general rule, heart specialists do not write about foot disease). This is also the case in other areas of the academy. English professors and other members of the university academy write primarily in the area to which they have devoted long hours of study. In education, however, too often people profess and write in areas in which they have not contributed as researchers or studied in depth. We value colleagues in special education, educational leadership, and those who study substantive instructional areas such as literacy, mathematics, science education, and technology who also value the role of expert knowledge. However, there are a number of people who consider themselves general instruction and curriculum theorists who extend their "knowledge base" too widely (and not too wisely?).

Critics outside the field of educational psychology have invested a great deal of interest in devaluing the role of research, theory, and empirical information possessed by the field. Some critics of educational psychology are avowed advocates of personal story and personal voice. Integrating the personal stories of participants when they add perspective and insight to fundamental issues of practice and theory is a good addition to the research methods for clarifying perceptions and performance. Indeed, much good work has been done in this area (see Goodson, 1997). However, when story is used to supplant research, theory, and empirical evidence,

Requests for reprints should be sent to Thomas L. Good, Department of Educational Psychology, University of Arizona, P.O. Box 210069, Tucson, AZ 85721. E-mail: tgood@mail.ed.arizona.edu

[1] Some of the 1996 issue focused on the relevance of educational psychology for teacher education and how to improve the teaching of educational psychology in teacher education programs. Here, we focus on the more general case of the relevance of educational psychology for educational practice.

rather than to supplement it, we have serious reservations about its value. Clearly, a story and its voice are not interesting per se—hundreds of books and articles are rejected each year because they lack style, substance, veracity, or value. Some stories are knowingly distorted and used for self-justification and self-enhancement.

This is not an argument to discourage honest debate and criticism. Criticisms from both within and outside the field offer ways to sharpen issues and to identify new directions. However, our point is to recognize the role of scholarship and knowledge. Too much time has been wasted in educational reform through the provision of new panaceas that have little theoretical coherence or empirical support. The heart of work in educational psychology is to produce theoretical and well-researched psychological knowledge that has the potential for enhancing learning and socialization in various settings. Hence, the field is interested in recruiting students who want to bring empirical data to support, reject, or transform new conceptions and theoretical stances.

LOST OPPORTUNITY

Educational research has been given a bad name largely because much of what is paraded as knowledge by educators is more anecdote and opinion than careful conceptualization, evidence, and measured attainments (e.g., see Levin & O'Donnell, 1999). The field needs to be more assertive in separating stories and good ideas from rigorous research and evidence. Given the considerable national interest in improving public education, it is important to begin to respond to issues of practice with theory and data.

One of the real consequences of failed school reform is that it erodes confidence in educational research because policymakers erroneously assume that educational reform is based on solid research evidence. Given the habit of the field to move rapidly from one panacea to another zeitgeist, it is likely that many policymakers will conclude the research base must be shallow. Hence, policymakers are increasingly unwilling to invest in needed basic research. Others too have lamented the lost opportunity for educational research.

> The benefits of research reform efforts are not fully realized in part because education research has not been organized, funded, and utilized as research in other important fields of public policy (National Research Council, 1999, p. 268).

THE COMPLEXITY OF EDUCATIONAL RESEARCH

Work in educational psychology has been evident by careful laboratory research that has yielded complex concepts relating to student learning, motivation, and other affective dispositions. Such work has yielded hypotheses for improving educational practice. In some cases, principles developed in laboratory settings are applicable in the classroom. Other concepts yield problematic value for application.

Some have attacked the field of educational psychology because the careful delineation and measurement of variables does not transform schooling in immediate, visible ways. Thus, in part, educational psychology has been dismissed because it fails to achieve the (inappropriate) expectations attributed to it by its critics. There are no magic bullets or instantaneous panaceas in education. The expectation that research can yield simple universal solutions is an untenable premise. When does a research finding matter? We have inferential statistical procedures to assess the extent to which a finding is not merely a chance occurrence and we have standardized metrics for assessing the extent to which a series of findings is associated with small or large "effects." Further, we have ways to consider the value of research findings both through theoretical analysis and replicated research. However, in the final analysis, the measurement of either teaching or learning outcomes in a classroom context (or in other naturalistic settings, such as a museum setting), where countless variables are operating and interacting, is a daunting task. Classrooms are as much about lost opportunity as they are about what actually occurred. Through thoughtful, systematic research investigations, plausible inferences can be made about teacher or classroom effects on students. Yet, even with careful measurements, the relation between teacher practices (instructional methods, curriculum assignments, etc.) and student performance is difficult to estimate. First, there is never a chance to observe or measure everything or to experience what a child experiences in the classroom or school setting. Moreover, even if one achieves a model program of research (random assignment of classrooms to instructional methods, "as intended" implementation of methods and measures, etc.), at best the research can assess the effects of an instructional intervention at one given point in time. There are infinite ways in which teachers and students could spend a school day or a school year. Hence, the theoretical effects of teaching and learning environments on students will continue to be a context for exciting and complex debate.

WHAT EDUCATIONAL RESEARCH YIELDS

Educational research cannot produce definitive answers. However, it can provide working concepts, language, data, and hypotheses that allow for the investigation of various possibilities (e.g., How does a reduction in class size affect social communication and subsequent student achievement?). Further, research can rule out certain approaches as being ineffective and suggest plausible hypotheses about promising new ones. Research can determine which instructional method, for which students, for which educational outcomes, makes more of a difference in a given context. Still, it is possible that other instructional formats—even radically different formats—might have produced more important accomplishments in the same amount of time.

Research that educational psychologists conduct is potentially very important. At the same time, it must be recognized that conducting classroom-based research is not a simple process. A given experiment or naturalistic study can consume enormous amounts of time in reviewing the literature, developing appropriate methods and instrumentation, collecting data, processing and analyzing data in appropriate ways, and arguing about various interpretations of data and their potential value.

Educational psychologists have concerns about evidence quality and intellectual integrity in research of all types, including experimental interventions, correlational studies, surveys and interviews, case studies, and observational research. In general, the field does not worship a single method, but tends to ask about the appropriateness of a given method in relation to a given question. At different stages of the research process and for differing educational prescriptions, some questions are best addressed by observation, others by interview or survey, and yet others by randomized "classroom trials" experiments (Levin & O'Donnell, 1999), or by various combinations of "quantitative" and "qualitative" approaches. We appeal to future educational psychology researchers to ply their trade with enthusiasm and with rigor, whether in laboratories, in field settings, or through archival review of policy documents.

THIS ISSUE

As the field of educational psychology moves into a new century, it is time to take stock of the field. Those who write in this issue affirm that the basic goals that the field has pursued for roughly the last 100 years—the development of theory and research to improve practice—has been and continues to be a noble enterprise. In this special issue of the *Educational Psychologist,* we provide but a limited sample of the past, present, and future of educational psychology. However, we hope the articles we assembled will stimulate a continuing dialogue about the role of educational psychology in promoting evidence-based knowledge that is of immense value for educational practice.

History

Angela O'Donnell and Joel Levin (2001) trace the evolution of educational psychology from its inception in the early 1900s to the present. They describe the rich conflicts and debates that have continuously marked the field, while pointing out that many of the early debates have endured throughout its history. It is important to recognize that they note that the field initially was stimulated by important differences in the conception of the two leading theorists at the time, Edward Thorndike and John Dewey, and that Thorndike's conception prevailed and continued to influence the direction of the field in important ways. Although the scope and essence of a discipline can be defined in various ways and through various archival documents, none are as central and sensitive as a review of the field's published research. O'Donnell and Levin illustrate that by providing a comprehensive examination of articles published in the *Journal of Educational Psychology* from 1910 to the present.

Contributions of Educational Psychology—Some Examples

Richard Mayer (2001) writes in support of the current and future robustness of educational psychology by noting its strengths and contributions in two areas—the psychology of subject matter and the teaching of cognitive strategies. His article provides compelling examples of how educational psychology has contributed to improving the school content areas of reading, mathematics, and history instruction. Unlike the dichotomous choices that some educators have urged about the value (or lack thereof) of educational psychology, Mayer argues that psychology and education are good for one another. By using the combined strengths of those two fields in strategic ways, educational psychology may improve both theories of instruction and instructional practice.

Scott Paris and Alison Paris (2001) document the contributions of educational psychology to the development of extensive research-based knowledge on students' self-regulated learning (SRL). In addition to detailing the rich history of the evolution of SRL (i.e., one's ability to direct, reflect on, and to engage in strategic learning), Paris and Paris highlight the continuing discussion in the field about how best to conceptualize SRL: as a set of skills to be taught, on the one hand, or as a developmental process to be realized, on the other, with the authors' preferred conceptualization to be the latter.

Edmund Emmer and Laura Stough (2001) trace the rich history of research on classroom management. They demonstrate that the field has been able to identify key management variables, both in naturalistic studies and experimental classroom interventions. They provide useful illustrations of how good management varies with instructional goals and formats, while raising questions for future research.

Future Directions

The article by Thomas Good and Sharon Nichols (2001) blends the past contributions of educational psychology with a brief example of policy issues that educational psychologists are increasingly likely to address in the future. They trace the rich history of research on teacher (and student) expectations and illustrate how constructs and hypotheses developed in the laboratory can be tested in social settings. They call for the field to address the gap between the achievement scores of White and Black students by aggressively implementing an expectation intervention in first-grade classrooms serving Black students from low-income families. Good and Nichols note that this is but one area where extant knowledge could be provided to extant social issues, with beneficial effects (e.g., designing better summer schools).

Jerome D'Agostino (2001) presents a historical analysis of the field of program evaluation—its multiple definitions and its varying use of theory. D'Agostino argues that the practice of program evaluation would be improved in important ways by the more appropriate use of formal theory. In particular, he argues that program evaluation specialists would function more forcefully if they had expertise in substantive theories of educational psychology, including cognition, metacognition, development, and motivation. Hence, D'Agostino suggests the need for educational psychology programs to be more integrated.

Mary McCaslin and Daniel Hickey (2001) conclude the special issue by noting that the field of psychology has been in search of an identity since its inception. Hence, it is no surprise that educational psychology suffers similar, if not more acute, problems. They posit that contemporary societal interest in education offers a unique chance for educational psychologists to do important work in applied settings. McCaslin and Hickey then address the virtues of understanding and implementing a clear, more powerful, conception of the "sociohistoric" constructivism perspective. Most importantly, the authors' call on the field to consider its historical roots, to choose both Dewey and Thorndike, and to bring empirical data to social policy issues while continuing to address topics of historical research interest. This synthesis represents a potentially exciting way of combining the diverse interests of educational psychologists.

REFERENCES

Berliner, D., & Calfee, R. (Eds.). (1996). *Handbook of Educational Psychology.* New York: Macmillan.

Blumenfeld, P., & Anderson, L. (Eds.). (1996). Special issue of the Educational Psychologist: Teacher education and educational psychology. *Educational Psychologist, 31,* 1–4.

D'Agostino, J. V. (2001). Increasing the role of educational psychology theory in program development and evaluation. *Educational Psychologist, 36,* 127–132.

Doyle, W., & Carter, K. (1996). Educational psychology and the education of teachers: A reaction. *Educational Psychologist, 31,* 22–28.

Emmer, E. T., & Stough, L. M. (2001). Classroom management: A critical part of educational psychology, with implications for teacher education. *Educational Psychologist, 36,* 103–112.

Good, T. L., & Nichols, S. L. (2001). Expectancy effects in the classroom: A special focus on improving the reading performance of minority students in first-grade classrooms. *Educational Psychologist, 36,* 113–126.

Goodson, I. (1997). The life and work of teachers. In B. Biddle, T. Good., & I. Goodson (Eds.), *International handbook of teachers and teaching* (pp. 135–152). Dordrecht, The Netherlands: Kluwer.

Levin, J. R., & O'Donnell, A. M. (1999). What to do about educational research's credibility gaps? *Issues in Education: Contributions From Educational Psychology, 5,* 177–229.

Mayer, R. E. (2001). What good is educational psychology? The case of cognition and instruction. *Educational Psychologist, 36,* 83–88.

McCaslin, M., & Hickey, D. T. (2001). Educational psychology, social constructivism, and educational practice: A case of emergent identity. *Educational Psychologist, 36,* 133–140.

National Research Council. (1999). *Improving student learning: A strategic plan for education research and its utilization. Committee on a Feasibility Study for Strategic Education Research Program. Commission on Behavioral and Social Sciences in Education, National Research Council.* Washington, DC: National Academy Press.

O'Donnell, A. M., & Levin, J. R. (2001). Educational psychology's healthy growing pains. *Educational Psychologist, 36,* 73–82.

Paris, S. G., & Paris, A. H. (2001). Classroom applications of research on self-regulated learning. *Educational Psychologist, 36,* 89–101.

Wise, P. (1997). A difficult book to pick up or put down. *Contemporary Psychology, 42,* 983–985.

EDUCATIONAL PSYCHOLOGIST, *36*(2), 73–82

Educational Psychology's Healthy Growing Pains

Angela M. O'Donnell
Department of Educational Psychology
Rutgers University

Joel R. Levin
Department of Educational Psychology
University of Arizona

This article outlines the historical development of educational psychology as a discipline, its current issues and tensions, and new directions that might flow from both its history and current state. In providing this synopsis for students of educational psychology, the article examines how the discipline was originally conceptualized, how current debates are elaborations of previous debates, and how these pressures sustain the field. In an effort to understand what has changed in educational psychology since its formal inception, the article reviews the contents of the first volume of the *Journal of Educational Psychology* for each decade from 1910 to 1990, as well as the 1999 volume. An interesting pattern that emerges from this inspection of topics is the focus on developing adequate measurement tools before the study of new topics can be fully embraced and pursued. The article concludes that the current debates about methods, purposes, and intended contributions of the field of educational psychology generally reflect a healthy state of its being.

After almost a century of growing pains for the field of educational psychology, and now as we begin the 21st century, a legitimate question to ask is, "How are we doing?" In this article, directed at students of educational psychology, we outline the historical development of the discipline, its current issues and tensions, and new directions that might flow from both its history and current state.[1] Although we recognize that there will not be consensus among educational psychology scholars concerning the discipline's raison d'être and associated foci, we need to center our discussion by endorsing one prevalent view of the discipline. We consider educational psychology to include the development and application of psychological principles to education, as well as the adoption of psychological perspectives on education. Notably, this definition does not assume a linear progression from psychology to education. Current debates revolve around issues such as the nature and purpose of educational psychology; its status as a field, discipline, or subfield; methods used to generate knowledge; and the proper purpose of educational psychology. We will return to some of these issues later in the article.

Educational psychology developed as a field from its initial beginnings under Edward L. Thorndike. In 1946, it became one of the original divisions of the American Psychological Association (APA). The divisions of APA were deemed to be sufficiently different from one another to warrant separate identities. In the 1940s, when members of the APA were surveyed about what they considered to be important concerns for psychologists, they indicated that psychology in education was a key concern. In the period 1948 to 1950, the *Journal of Educational Psychology* devoted many of its pages to issues of application of psychology to education, particularly to teacher education. Despite periods of difficulty (see Grinder, 1989), educational psychology maintains a strong presence within APA at this time. The influence of educational psychology is evident in APA's publication of learner-centered principles and a series of books on psychology in the schools—for example, see Zimmerman, Bonner, and Kovak's (1996) book, *Developing Self-Regu-*

Requests for reprints should be sent to Angela M. O'Donnell, Department of Educational Psychology, Rutgers University, 10 Seminary Place, New Brunswick, NJ 08901–1183. E-mail: angelao@rci.rutgers.edu

[1]In recent years, a number of issues of the *Educational Psychologist* (the official journal of the American Psychological Association's educational psychology division, Division 15) have been devoted to considering the current status of educational psychology as a discipline. In addition, many of the major figures in educational psychology have commented on the future of the discipline (e.g., Calfee, 1992; Klausmeier, 1988; Mayer, 1992; Pintrich, 1994; Wittrock, 1994; Woolfolk Hoy, 1996).

lated Learners: Beyond Achievement to Self-Efficacy. Work such as this is strongly influenced by knowledge generated through educational psychology research, suggesting that the field is alive and well, contributing in important ways to both educational practice and psychological theory.

When one considers the apparent conflicts in the field as evidenced by the current debates, one might be tempted to conclude that educational psychology has outlived its usefulness. We argue that such a conclusion is not justified. The broader field of education is also fraught with conflicts about appropriate purposes, methods, and connections between educational practitioners and academic researchers', conflicts that are paralleled in other contemporary academic disciplines as well (Levin & O'Donnell, 1999). Certainly, it is true that educational psychology as a discipline is in the process of reconsidering its mission. Rather than seeing this as a negative, however, we regard a consideration of purpose, method, and intended contributions to be an encouraging sign of a discipline that is addressing the challenges posed by a changing society (see also Mayer, 2001).

AN HISTORICAL JOURNEY THROUGH THE FIELD OF EDUCATIONAL PSYCHOLOGY

Framed against a backdrop of the historical development of the field of educational psychology, the current debates about purpose, content, and methods seem to mark developmental milestones of a developing field. Our view of educational psychology is strongly influenced by its psychological component and one that has its origin (but not termination) in the work of Thorndike, rather than that of Dewey. According to Hilgard (1996), E. L. Thorndike's (1903) book, *Educational Psychology*, defined the field. Hilgard identified Thorndike and Dewey as two central figures that shaped educational psychology in the early years of the century. The positions represented by these two figures illustrate some of the key differences in perspective on educational psychology. Although both men valued science as the road to knowledge, Thorndike was an experimenter whereas Dewey was not. Dewey was concerned about the politics and social context of education whereas Thorndike was not. These two positions do not reflect polarities (Hilgard, 1996) but reflect different emphases on the "education" and "psychology" aspects of educational psychology (see also McCaslin & Hickey, 2001).

At a broader "bidisciplinary" level, researchers and theorists in educational psychology are aligned more with either education or psychology. One tension in educational psychology is associated with a focus on one or the other side of its broad bidisciplinarity, a tension that has its historical roots in the key differences of focus of Dewey and Thorndike. This distinction tends to be aligned with the emphases on practical applications (improving schools), on the one hand, or on theory development and testing (understanding behavior), on the other. These respective emphases are not necessarily mutually exclusive, although they are often perceived to be so (see, for example, Berliner, 1992, p. 158).

In the inaugural issue of the *Journal of Educational Psychology*, E. L. Thorndike (1910) addressed this relation in an essay entitled, "The Contribution of Psychology to Education." In his essay, Thorndike described what he believed to be the possible contributions of psychology to education, the essential role that psychology could play, the mutual influence of education and psychology, and recognition of varied methods of study. This early writing on the contribution of psychology to education still has relevance; and the topics, content, and methods described by Thorndike remain among those that provoke controversy today.

Educational Psychology at the Beginning

According to Thorndike (1910), education is concerned with "changes in the intellects, characters, and behaviors of men, its problems being roughly included under these four topics: Aims, materials, means, and methods" (p. 5). Thorndike believed that psychology could contribute to each of these four areas of problems. It could make educational aims clearer and measure the probability that the aim is attainable. Thorndike claimed that psychology was the main contributor to the "material" (1910, p. 6) of education. If education promotes change in the intellect, character, and behavior of people, psychology is the science that provides "thinkers and workers in the field of education (e.g., teachers) with knowledge of the material with which they work" (1910, p. 6). The task of providing such knowledge is shared by other disciplines.

Thorndike also noted that psychology could contribute to methods of teaching in three ways. First, psychology could deduce methods from the laws of human nature. Second, even when teaching methods were chosen from actual working experience without reference to psychology (i.e., when teachers operated out of intuition or belief), psychology could be helpful in explaining why particular methods succeeded, and thus could lead "the way to new insights regarding other questions not settled by experience" (Thorndike, 1910, p. 7). Third, because of its procedures for measuring knowledge and skill, psychology could also suggest means of testing, verifying, or refuting the claims of any teaching method.[2] Thus, in the early part of the century and in the inaugural issue of the *Journal of Educational Psychology*, the principal founder of educational psychology as a discipline noted the interdisciplinary nature of education and the important contribution of psychology to some of the key tasks of education (teaching, in particular).

---

[2]As an important "measurement" aside and a theme to which we return throughout the article, Thorndike (1910) noted that three quarters of the problems of educational practice are problems about "amounts" (p. 8) and that psychology could contribute special knowledge to such quantification.

Thorndike (1910) observed that some key aspects of human functioning were less frequently studied than were such topics as the unlearned response tendencies of ants and chickens. He noted that the "extreme complexity and intimate mixture with habits in the case of human instincts prevents studies of them, even when made with great care, from giving entirely unambiguous and elegant results" (p. 10). In a foreshadowing of the kind of methodological divergence that emerged and was debated heatedly in subsequent decades, Thorndike (1910) made the following observations about the appropriate methods and attitudes for conducting research:

> The educational theorist or practitioner who should conclude that his casual observations of children in homes and schools needs no reinforcement from the researches of psychologists would be making the same sort of, though not so great, an error as the pathologist or physician who should neglect the scientific studies of bacteria and protozoa. Also the psychologist who condemns these studies in toto because they lack the precision and surety of his own studies of the sensations and perceptual judgments is equally narrow, though from a better motive. (pp. 10–11)

Thorndike (1910) anticipated that future issues of the *Journal of Educational Psychology* would include articles reporting research from both laboratories and schools. His essential belief in the importance of both laboratory and school-based work is also clear in the following excerpt:

> The science of education can and will itself contribute abundantly to psychology. Not only do laws derived by psychology from simple, specially arranged experiments help us to interpret and control mental action under the conditions of school-room life. School-room life itself is a vast laboratory in which there are made thousands of experiments of the utmost interest to "pure psychology." (p. 12)

Thorndike (1910, p. 12) expected action in the world to be accompanied by "truth about the world" and such truth to eventually lead to action in the world. Thus, one of the founders of educational psychology recognized the importance of all of the following: classroom-based research, individual differences, precise methodology, the contribution of other kinds of methodological approaches beyond those applied in laboratories, and the relation between understanding of phenomena and action in the world. Some of the criticisms currently being directed toward the discipline of educational psychology are precisely about these issues.

We do not mean to imply that other authors in the early part of the century did not contribute to the defining of educational psychology. However, many of the key issues identified by Thorndike in his 1910 article have reverberated throughout the 20th century and still pose interesting challenges (e.g., the relations among laboratory research, classroom research, and classroom practice). If the issues identified by Thorndike near the beginning of the 20th century remain of concern as we enter the 21st, what has occurred in the interim? In the following section, we examine the topical shifts in educational psychology as represented in the *Journal of Educational Psychology* since 1910. Although other journals predate this journal (e.g., *Teachers College Record*), the *Journal of Educational Psychology* is one of the first to focus on educational psychology in its own right.[3]

Research Topics in Educational Psychology: 1910 to the Present

In an effort to understand what has changed in the field of educational psychology since its formal inception, we reviewed the first volume of the *Journal of Educational Psychology* for each decade from 1910 to 1990, as well as the 1999 volume (for related reviews, see Ball, 1984, and Walberg & Haertel, 1992). A total of 641 articles were examined and although the sample is not exhaustive, it is at least illustrative. We focused on the *Journal of Educational Psychology* as one of the longest running and most influential journals in the area and one that is associated with the professional organization of psychology, the APA. The empirical research reported in the journal is generally of high quality. The intent of this summary is to provide a sketch of what changes have occurred in the last century. The methods used in a discipline reflect the worldview espoused by investigators in that discipline (Guba & Lincoln, 1994).

Topic identification and classification. For each article considered, we attempted to characterize its major topic. If an article included a variety of topics, we classified the article in terms of its central theme. For example, we classified articles about the reliability of student evaluations of college teaching as measurement articles because the key research issue was one of measurement. We do not make strong claims for the "validity" of these categories but they serve a useful descriptive function. By comparing our general categories with those reported in Ball's (1984) similar *Journal of Educational Psychology* content analysis between 1910 and 1980, we can claim at least some face validity for the kinds of categories, topics, and distributional patterns that emerged.

Eight general article categories were selected: (a) Intelligence Tests and Relation of Intelligence to Other Variables; (b) Tests and Measurement; (c) Learning; (d) Teaching; (e) Motivation; (f) Attitudes, Affect, and Personality; (g) Behavior; and (h) Other. Category 1, *Intelligence Tests and Relation of Intelligence to Other Variables,* included arti-

[3]Also at the turn of the 20th century, the *Elementary School Journal* (started in 1900 at the University of Chicago) reflected the influence of John Dewey and accordingly provided more of an education than a psychology emphasis.

cles about measuring intelligence, developing IQ tests, and relating intelligence to other variables of interest, such as gender or achievement. Articles were placed in this category if their primary focus was on intelligence. Category 2, *Tests and Measurement,* included a variety of types of content. Articles placed in this category focused primarily on issues of reliability or validity, instrument development, and other measurement issues. Articles on the evaluation of teaching and variables that may compromise the reliability and validity of such evaluations were also placed in this category.

Articles classified as *Learning* (Category 3) focused primarily on influencing some outcome measure related to learning. Many learning articles included instructional variables or text manipulations. Although learning and teaching are hard to separate, articles were classified as *Teaching* (Category 4) if they dealt primarily with teacher behavior. Articles classified as *Motivation* (Category 5) were mainly about the influence of motivation, constructs such as test anxiety, student efficacy, learned helplessness, and the measurement of these constructs, or the relation of motivation to other variables. Articles from more recent decades often incorporated a variety of variables into studies of motivation (including achievement outcomes), but the article was classified as Motivation if the primary emphasis was on motivation as explanation or as an object of study. Articles on students' attitudes, self-esteem, self-concept, and personality variables were assigned to *Attitudes, Affect, and Personality* (Category 6). Articles pertaining to students' classroom behavior (including that of students diagnosed as learning disabled, emotionally disturbed, and having attention deficit hyperactivity disorder) were classified as *Behavior* (Category 7). Articles placed in the *Other* category (Category 8) included both general policy-issue statements, commentaries, and notes that could not be unambiguously classified in terms of their primary topic of study, as well as editorials and introductions to special sections of the *Journal of Educational Psychology*.

The categories we developed are necessarily general and we do not provide an in-depth analysis of the variation within each category. For example, views of learning have changed considerably between 1910 and 1999. The variation in view is not captured by our categories but the categories used provide a general characterization of changes in emphases in the field. Concerning the intrajudge stability of these classifications, the first author classified the articles from 1960, 1970, and 1980 on two different occasions (separated by an interval of a year). The between-occasions correlation of the number of articles assigned to the eight categories (the seven major categories plus the Other category) was .96. In Table 1, we present the percentage of articles published in a given volume that were assigned to each of the eight categories.[4]

[4]Ball's (1984) analysis produced 13 categories, and so our 8 would appear to be defined somewhat more globally.

1910. In the first (1910) volume of the *Journal of Educational Psychology*, a total of 30 articles were published. Of those 30, 6 (20%) fell into the Other category (e.g., an analysis of courses in education offered at a German university). Almost none of the 20 empirical studies used any sort of statistical analysis but rather were characterized by observation; several of the articles consisted of "reflections" on strategies needed for instruction. Four and nine articles were concerned with learning and teaching, respectively. In 1910, no articles were published in the areas of motivation, attitudes, or personality concerns.

Many of the topics that are of interest today were also of interest in 1910. For example, there were articles on "the college laggard" (today, the "underachieving" or "poorly motivated" student) and on the "qualities of merit in teachers." A number of articles commented on the importance of practical experience as necessary to learning well in college classrooms. Thus, even this early in the 20th century, there was some press for authentic tasks. The unavailability of good measures of intellectual functioning or learning outcomes limited the kind of work that could be produced.

Thorndike noted in his article in the 1910 inaugural issue of the *Journal of Educational Psychology* that one of the key concerns that people of the time had was whether differential amounts of money invested in a child's education could produce differential outcomes: "Just how much more does a boy learn when thirty dollars a year is spent for his teaching than when only twenty dollars is spent?" (Thorndike, 1910, p. 8). Although the specific dollar amounts may change, along with gender and other demographically relevant concerns, Thorndike's basic question remains the same. That is, despite antipathy in certain current circles toward measuring, quantifying, or counting, the question posed by Thorndike some 90 years ago addresses a fundamental public policy issue in the United States today.

Concerning measurement as a topic of study, in 1910 Thorndike suggested that one way in which psychology could contribute to the theory and practice of education was through the discovery and improvement of means of measurement of intellectual functions. A second line of work identified by Thorndike as having special significance concerned race, age, gender, and individual differences as they influenced "intellect, character, and behavior" (p. 8). A key question in exploring individual differences was the degree to which "intellectual and moral differences found in human beings are consequences of their original nature and determined by the ancestry from which they spring" (p. 9). Although Thorndike signaled the importance of measurement and individual differences, in the 1910 volume of the *Journal of Educational Psychology* there was little attention to those topics.

1920. All this was to change by 1920, however. At that time, the largest percentage of articles (44%) was in the area of tests and measurement. Combined with articles on intelli-

TABLE 1
Percentage Distribution of Topics of Study in Selected Volumes of the *Journal of Educational Psychology* (1910–1999)

Topic	*1910*	*1920*	*1930*	*1940*	*1950*	*1960*	*1970*	*1980*	*1990*	*1999*
Intelligence tests–relation to intelligence	13.3	18.0	9.5	23.9	10.0	5.2	0.0	3.2	0.0	0.0
Tests and measurement	23.3	43.6	54.1	46.3	35.0	29.3	8.3	18.3	9.5	10.0
Learning	13.3	18.0	14.9	19.4	12.5	25.9	62.5	41.9	41.0	60.0
Teaching	30.0	2.6	2.7	3.0	7.5	12.1	1.4	11.8	3.8	3.0
Motivation	0.0	15.4	1.4	4.5	0.0	1.7	9.7	9.7	18.1	10.0
Attitude–affect–personality	0.0	0.0	5.4	3.0	12.5	20.7	16.7	9.7	16.2	14.0
Behavior	0.0	0.0	0.0	0.0	5.0	3.5	0.0	3.2	1.9	3.0
Other	20.0	2.6	12.2	0.0	17.5	1.7	1.4	2.2	9.5	0.0
Number of articles	30	39	74	67	40	58	72	93	105	63

gence testing, more than 60% of the 39 articles published in this volume were about measurement of individual difference variables in intellectual functioning. The increase in work in this area coincided with the introduction to the United States of Binet's intelligence test. Measurement of other individual difference variables (e.g., motivation) was also the subject of investigation (15%). Thorndike had noted the paucity of measures of intellectual functioning and until such measures were developed, very little about such functioning could be assessed or mediated.

1930 and 1940. The emphasis on measurement continued in 1930 and 1940. Thorndike (1910) had noted that psychologists' ability to measure complex constructs was a vital activity. The topic of learning received relatively little attention in the *Journal of Educational Psychology* in 1930. When learning was the object of study, the kind of learning examined was often motor development (e.g., handwriting). It would seem that such learning took precedence because it was measurable and could be measured with accuracy. The year 1940 saw the continuance of an emphasis on measurement, identification, and selection through the use of tests, IQ measures, and so forth. Research on affective characteristics or motivation was negligible.

1950. In 1947, the Executive Committee of the National Society of College Teachers organized several committees to study the various aspects of teacher education. One of these committees had responsibility for recommending the content, sequence, organization, and teaching procedures for courses in educational psychology. In the 1950 issue of the *Journal of Educational Psychology*, there were six articles on the content of educational psychology that might be necessary in a program of teacher preparation (in the Other category). A previous volume of the journal had included five articles on the nature of educational psychology and the contributions it both had made and could make to the preparation of teachers.

In the 1950 volume of the *Journal of Educational Psychology*, measurement issues were concerned with identification and selection. Personality traits also became an important area of study, whereas studies in intelligence testing declined in number.

It is evident from an examination of Table 1 that research published in the *Journal of Educational Psychology* from 1920 to 1950 was heavily weighted in the direction of measurement, testing, and prediction. When Thorndike (1910) wrote his introductory article in the *Journal of Educational Psychology*, very few tools were available for the measurement of intellectual functioning. The arrival of Binet's IQ test in this country stimulated a great deal of work on efforts to provide better measurement. From 1910 to 1950, two World Wars shook the world and major mobilizations of the army and other forces placed a vigorous effort on measurement and selection processes. This early work was characterized by a focus on the development of instruments, rigorous measurement of constructs, and a focus on construct validation. Some efforts were also directed at measuring the capacity and function of memory, and using tasks such as recalling nonsense syllables and learning word lists. The goal of much of this work was to understand the causes of human behavior and functioning, and this resulted in the adoption of methods designed to identify causal relations and to rule out alternative explanations.

1960 and 1970. The most even distribution across topics of study was found in the 1960 volume of the journal. In 1970, the largest category of study was Learning, with the focus of investigation typically on small informational units (i.e., processes and strategies involved in learning words, sentences, or paragraphs). Attention was also directed toward basic processes in reading. A large emphasis was similarly placed on programmed instruction and how to manage it. It is important to remember that little was known at that time about basic cognitive structures and processes. The advent of reliable (and thought-to-be valid) measuring instruments made the study of these structures and processes possible. Research on intelligence was very scarce in 1970, which may have been attributable in part to both the discipline and society in general beginning to afford greater recognition to the influence of environmental factors on human intellectual functioning (see also Good & Nichols, 2001).

1980 and the 1990s. An emphasis on learning research continued in 1980 and through the 1990s. However, the specific topics of investigation changed considerably from the 1970s, with attention given to cognitive processes and "higher order" information processing, metacognition, strategic learning, and interactions of learning with task instructions or media. Teaching, per se, has not attracted a lot of attention, although interest in teaching is somewhat masked by the category structure employed in Table 1. A number of articles appeared on issues related to the reliability and validity of student evaluations of college teaching. The kinds of issues raised in the previously mentioned article, "The Qualities of Merit in Teachers" (Ruediger & Strayer, 1910), remain germane.

Comment

One interesting pattern that emerges from an inspection of the topics of study throughout the past century is the focus on developing adequate measurement tools before the study of new topics could be well developed. Achievement and intellectual functioning could not be studied until measures of functioning could be developed and trusted. Influences of motivational constructs could not be interpreted until reliable measures of motivation could be validated. Thus, attention to measurement seems to precede a deepening of the complexity of phenomena that can be entertained as objects of study—see also Tweney and Budzynski's (2000) discussion of the "measurement" issue in their historical examination of the field of psychology as a whole.

As inroads in understanding of intellectual functioning were made, new challenges in understanding the role of affective influences in educational achievement were posed. In the latter part of the century, a growing interest in motivational and attitudinal issues is evident in the articles published in the *Journal of Educational Psychology*.[5] New journals were initiated that specialized in statistics and measurement and the appearance of these journals diminished the need for the *Journal of Educational Psychology* to be an outlet for advances in these areas. A variety of other new journals in the areas of learning, cognition, and development have also appeared in that interval.

A recent survey covering the period 1991 to 1996 (Smith et al., 1998) serves to corroborate and extend (across four other educational psychology journals) both the general recent-times topical emphases and the earlier-to-recent-times topical shifts that we encountered:

> Reading, learning, achievement, assessment of student learning, human development, motivation, mathematics education, and issues related to the identity of the field of educational psychology represent the most frequently published topics. Other topics that, in earlier times, have often been the focus of educational psychology research were represented relatively infrequently. (p. 178)

As a discipline, educational psychology has changed greatly since its inception. Scholars in recent years have written extensively about the nature of educational psychology as they attempt to encourage change or grapple with change. The ongoing tensions between education and psychology with respect to the discipline of educational psychology have resulted in criticisms of the discipline. In many respects, the current tensions evident in educational psychology are strongly rooted in the past concerns of the educational psychology, perhaps most clearly delineated in Thorndike's 1910 article on the contribution of psychology to education.

CRITICISMS OF EDUCATIONAL PSYCHOLOGY

In this section, we describe some of the general criticisms of educational psychology made by Grinder (1989) and characterize some specific instances of differences among researchers in educational psychology that have provoked criticism. Grinder described educational psychology as having three major and overlapping problems: withdrawal, fractionation, and irrelevance (see also Calfee & Berliner, 1996; Elkind, 1999). Grinder noted that as early as 1948, educational psychologists were known to withdraw from any responsibility for education, retreating into "the more limited fields of experimental psychology" (p. 14). This was not what Thorndike had envisioned for the field almost 40 years before that. Other expressions of this disconnection include criticisms of educational psychology "foundational" courses that were quite separate from general teacher preparation (Anderson et al., 1995). The current state of educational psychology cannot legitimately be characterized as "withdrawal" in that educational psychologists have contributed to the APA series on *Psychology in the Schools* and more and more researchers conduct classroom-based research. The debates about the purposes of educational psychology have no doubt contributed to this change.

Grinder (1989) considered the problem of *fractionation* to be a critical problem in a field that he characterized as "withdrawn" and "disconnected." He criticized educational psychology for lacking a connection to practical matters (e.g., authentic classroom processes), a criticism that was similarly

[5] Citizens—especially parents—are increasingly asking schools to meet the "nonsubject matter" needs of students. Educational psychologists are likely to make major contributions to this by developing appropriate measuring instruments (e.g., Rothstein, 2000).

expressed more recently by Anderson et al. (1995). The lack of common ground among academic educational psychologists is one that has existed since 1950 (Grinder, 1989). The associated tensions inherent in a lack of common ground go back much further than that, however, and the sources of this kind of fractionation were anticipated by Thorndike (1910) when he distinguished between action and understanding, between casual observation and precise measurement, and between research in school classrooms and research in university laboratories. The tensions anticipated by Thorndike are evident in current discussions of whether the appropriate focus of educational psychology is to improve schools or to understand schooling.

The lack of common ground is not surprising when one considers the diverse training that people who identify as educational psychologists may have. Some receive their training in schools of education whereas others are trained in psychology departments. Some have classroom teaching experiences, others do not. Some see the role of educational psychology as mainly about teacher preparation, others consider teacher preparation as one venue for the expression of educational psychological knowledge. Depending on the experiences, training, and beliefs that people bring to the table, conceptualizations of the proper role of educational psychology (improving schools, generating knowledge, or both) will vary. One only has to sit down with colleagues to develop a set of required readings in educational psychology to gain a glimpse of quite large differences in belief about the substance of the discipline. The diversity of initial training experienced by educational psychologists and their subsequent involvement in educational practice does not easily lend itself to cohesion of purposes.

As we recently noted (Levin & O'Donnell, 1999), research in educational psychology is often characterized by its critics as reductionistic, failing to capture the essential complexity of human behavior in context. Such research is criticized for lacking external validity or purpose. Criticisms of what might be called "molecular empiricist methodologies" have been frequent. Perhaps the underlying criticism leveled at this type of psychological research is that human behavior cannot be reduced to simple behaviors for which there are causal explanations.

The value of the knowledge base derived from laboratory research has been criticized, occasionally in ways that deny what has been learned from laboratory research—for example, the vast yield that (mostly) laboratory research has produced regarding the basic mechanisms and factors associated with human information processing (perception, comprehension, memory, and problem solving). This knowledge of human memory and problem solving has important implications for classroom learning (e.g., see Mayer, 2001). Making that knowledge accessible to those who might use it (e.g., classroom teachers) has been problematic.

The field of educational psychology has made substantial progress in the study of individuals. We have learned a great deal about basic structures and processes of individual cognition. The strategies for doing so have included rigorous experimentation, the development of causal models, and the construction of testable theories. Some would regard this approach as being too remote from classrooms. However, more basic research has had important classroom implications. For example, in his chapter, "The seven ages of working memory," Logie (1994) described how the concept of working memory has evolved from working memory as a "contemplation" of a retrieved memory to one of working memory as a workplace. Advances in understanding this most fundamental aspect of human cognition have occurred as a result of controlled laboratory research, often with "meaningless" stimulus materials. If research must necessarily be classroom-based and involve authentic tasks to be considered appropriate or useful, then the work conducted on working memory would fail to meet these criteria. However, this work has generated knowledge that is powerfully useful in the classroom. Knowledge of working memory has been used to understand a number of critical classroom concerns such as the cognitive demands of writing (Torrance & Jeffrey, 1999) and the difficulties experienced by learning-disabled children (Hulme & MacKenzie, 1992). Research that seemed so adrift of practical issues of classrooms can contribute in important ways to solving practical problems in classrooms, even if not immediately. The example of working memory is only one example of many that could be used to illustrate the point that basic research can lead to valuable applications (for a social–psychological example, see Good & Nichols, 2001).

A vision of the mutual influence of classroom and laboratory was first articulated by Thorndike in 1910. The realization of this vision requires that we recognize that the contribution of scientific work is not always immediately understood, that reassessment of what has been learned from research is often selective, and that progress requires that we continue to seek new questions in classroom problems and contexts as well as in laboratory situations. In our view, when framed within the evolution of the discipline, current debates about the nature of educational psychology (e.g., Anderson et al., 1995; Doyle & Carter, 1996; Pintrich, 1994; Woolfolk Hoy, 1996) and how "learning" should be conceptualized and studied (e.g., Anderson, Reder, & Simon, 1996; Greeno, 1997) can be interpreted more as a healthy bridge to its future than as a tomb for its past.

The Lure of Authenticity

The bulk of recent writings about the nature and appropriate content and focus in educational psychology encourages (even demands) that research be conducted in classrooms. Klausmeier (1988) argued for research in classrooms and noted that the classroom would be the new laboratory, just as Ausubel (1968) argued a generation earlier. Such research would generate knowledge that is valid in the sense of its describing, explaining, or guiding the processes of schooling. Classroom-based research could also test the usability of knowledge generated by psychologists in nonschool settings.

Thus, and in light of the preceding backdrop, educational psychology research has been criticized because it does not inform practice. Moreover, it is not just laboratory-derived research findings that are regarded as inapplicable to matters of classroom learning and instruction. Slavin (1996) noted that teachers are reluctant to use mechanisms for individual accountability when using cooperative learning in classrooms, although he points to a large body of research that identifies the presence of this feature of a cooperative learning environment as crucial to promoting achievement. All of Slavin's work on cooperative learning has been conducted in classrooms. Antil, Jenkins, Wayne, and Vadasy (1998) found that although their sample of elementary school teachers were knowledgeable about various methods of cooperative learning, very few of them used the techniques as they were intended or in the ways that the research on their efficacy had shown them to be important. Thus, although the research base for recommendations about the use of cooperative learning is "authentic" (i.e., it was conducted in public school classrooms), the findings from such research are not used.[6]

Despite the lure of relevance associated with authentic contexts, it is difficult to attribute student outcomes to instructional methods or materials in such contexts. "Design experiments" (Brown, 1992; Collins, 1992) are an attempt to study cognitive processes and behaviors in authentic contexts such as classrooms. The advantages of such approaches include attempting to understand phenomena in the complex situations in which they occur. Typically, many variables are manipulated in "experiments" that are conducted in one or a few classrooms and are characterized by their lack of commonly accepted standards of scientific credibility (Levin & O'Donnell, 1999). Thus, when a certain instructional intervention appears to work, it is difficult (if not impossible) to know why it works—in particular, what the critical and generalizable elements of the intervention are, as opposed to the optional, irrelevant, and classroom-specific ones. Such concerns become paramount if one is concerned about making inferences about the instructional intervention's potential in other similar classrooms. Concern for external (over internal) validity, consideration of the complexity of human behavior, and the emergence of sociocultural theory as part of the theoretical fabric of understanding educational processes, have resulted in the widespread adoption of more "qualitative" approaches.

[6]In addition, although a focus on "classroom learning" is important, an exclusive focus on it as the only legitimate venue for research in educational psychology would be limiting. Nowadays, "learning" is not bounded by school walls or by teachers. The advent of the World Wide Web, the lengthening life span, the increased use of informal learning environments such as art galleries and museums, and the rapid changes in the workplace require that learning occurs in a variety of contexts and across time and space.

Summary

Demands for educational psychology to be a field in which psychological principles are applied to educational practice are limiting (Wittrock, 1994). Current criticisms virtually insist that educational psychologists give up their theory-development efforts and work instead on "improving schooling." Thorndike's (1910) earlier description of the relation between truth in the world and action in the world was a call to educational psychology to do both. Wittrock (1994) reminds us of this dual obligation. It is an unfortunate consequence that E. L. Thorndike, who first wrote about the promise for reciprocal contributions of schools and laboratories, has come to be regarded by certain educational psychologists as the quintessential proponent of a reductionistic psychology derived from laboratory research (e.g., Calfee & Berliner, 1996).

The availability of alternative research methodologies highlights a key issue among educational psychologists regarding the purposes of their work and the location of their efforts. Some educational psychologists have argued that the only legitimate purpose of educational psychology is to improve schooling, although it is not clear how such a purpose can include a role for conducting research. Research methods that are often deemed appropriate for the pursuit of this goal include the use of design experiments, in which research is conducted in authentic contexts under flexible experimental requirements. Advocates of an educational psychology proposing to improve schooling criticize research conducted in laboratory settings as being decontextualized and irrelevant to natural contexts and the educational process. Alternatively, criticisms can be directed at research in more authentic contexts in terms of its inability to separate instructional-method effects from teacher-, student-, and classroom-related factors (because of the typical confounding of the former with the latter). Instructional methods and contexts are not, however, mutually exclusive. Knowledge from laboratory experiments can contribute to practice and contexts of practice can be studied using many different kinds of methodological approaches—including, especially, classroom-based instructional research that *does* permit scientifically credible conclusions (Levin, 1994; Levin & O'Donnell, 1999).

A GLIMPSE INTO THE FUTURE

Educational psychology is a field characterized by vigorous debates over the utility of alternative methods of research inquiry, the relation of theory and practice, the proper role of educational psychology in improving schooling or developing better theories, and the centrality or not of teacher education. These divisions of opinion about specifics seem to be skirmishes on the outer edge of a more central issue: Contemporary educational psychology does not have a single epistemological stance. Instead, it is characterized by two different research traditions: positivist or postpositivist, on the one hand, and critical theory and constructivism, on the other.

Positivist or postpositivist approaches to research are characterized by a focus on explanation, prediction, and control (Guba & Lincoln, 1994). This tradition, which has a long history in educational psychology, focuses on hypotheses and experiments. Critical theory or constructivism is concerned with arriving at greater understanding for both researchers and participants (Guba & Lincoln, 1994). Advocates of this viewpoint focus on more qualitative methods designed to guide understanding in specific, complex contexts. Tudge (2000) noted that the methods and analytical techniques relevant to one approach are "inappropriate for use by those whose work falls within a different theoretical perspective" (p. 100). The dilemma created by different traditions cannot be solved easily:

> It seems clear, therefore, that the worldview that one adopts has enormous implications for one's notion of reality, the type of theory that one finds appealing, the methods one uses, the way in which one analyzes and interprets the data. Not surprisingly, discussions of methodological and analytical differences cannot make much headway until differences at the paradigmatic and theoretical levels have been clarified. (Tudge, 2000, p. 100)

Current debates about where, when, and why educational psychology research should be conducted are more centrally a debate over epistemological approaches. Are researchers staying true to the epistemological position they have adopted when they choose methods, analytical techniques, and strategies for interpretation? The juxtaposition of two paradigms within a single subfield has promoted debate about our purposes and our methods. Among the key concepts in many branches of psychology is the notion that growth occurs through adaptation and that something must provoke that need to adapt (e.g., Piaget's notion of disequilibration and reequilibration, De Lisi & Golbeck, 1999). Thus, discussion and argument about the nature of educational psychology and its purposes seem more indicative of a healthy intellectual environment than a malady. Indeed, this internal debate within the field of educational psychology coincides with the field having more widespread influence in the general field of psychology than has occurred in decades.

Among the key questions to be addressed in the future is a return to the dilemma of what to include in graduate training in educational psychology. What relative weights should be given the two constituent terms, education and psychology? What are the appropriate substantive foci? What are the preferred methods of inquiry? Although Scheurman, Heeringa, Rocklin, and Lohman (1993) provided a description of what may appear to be relatively recent practices, their work preceded the period of more conscious inspection of the nature and purposes of educational psychology. It is not clear whether those practices emerged from reflections on the nature of the discipline and other issues that have been the subject of critical debate. As for educational psychology research, once again in our history it appears to be time to call for a "reciprocity treaty" of sorts. The reciprocal nature of theory development and practice that can occur between classrooms and research laboratories should be praised and promoted. This notion was present in the formative years of educational psychology as a discipline and is still being fueled by current debate. Reciprocity has the potential to enrich both our understanding of human learning and our ability to foster it.

ACKNOWLEDGMENTS

Part of this article was prepared while Joel R. Levin was a visiting scholar at the University of Arizona. He acknowledges the resources made available by the Department of Higher Education during that time, as well as the financial support for a leave provided by the Graduate School of the University of Wisconsin–Madison.

REFERENCES

Antil, L. R., Jenkins, J. R., Wayne, S. K., & Vadasy, P. F. (1998). Cooperative learning: Prevalence, conceptualizations, and the relationships between research and practice. *American Educational Research Journal, 3*, 419–455

Anderson, L. M., Blumenfeld, P., Pintrich, P. R., Clark, C. M., Marx, R. W., & Peterson, P. (1995). Educational psychology for teachers: Reforming our courses, rethinking our roles. *Educational Psychologist, 30*, 143–157.

Anderson, J. R., Reder, L. M., & Simon, H. A. (1996). Situated learning and education. *Educational Researcher, 25*(4), 5–11.

Ausubel, D. P. (1968, February). *Is there a discipline of educational psychology?* Paper presented at the annual meeting of the American Educational Research Association, Chicago.

Ball, S. (1984). Educational psychology as an academic chameleon: An editorial assessment after 75 years. *Journal of Educational Psychology, 76*, 993–999.

Berliner, D. C. (1992). Telling the stories of educational psychology. *Educational Psychologist, 27*, 143–161.

Brown, A. L. (1992). Design experiments: Theoretical and methodological challenges in creating complex interventions in classroom settings. *Journal of the Learning Sciences, 2*, 141–178.

Calfee, R. C. (1992). Rethinking educational psychology: The case of the missing links. *Educational Psychologist, 27*, 162–175.

Calfee, R. C., & Berliner, D. C. (1996). Introduction to a dynamic and relevant educational psychology. In D. C. Berliner & R. C. Calfee (Eds.), *Handbook of educational psychology* (pp. 1–11). New York: Macmillan.

Collins, A. (1992). Toward a design science of education. In E. Scanlon & T. O'Shea (Eds.), *New directions in educational technology* (pp. 15–22). New York: Springer-Verlag.

De Lisi, R., & Golbeck, S. (1999). Implications of Piagetian theory for peer learning. In A. M. O'Donnell & A. King (Eds.), *Cognitive perspectives on peer learning* (pp. 3–37). Mahwah, NJ: Lawrence Erlbaum Associates, Inc.

Doyle, W., & Carter, K. (1996). Educational psychology and the education of teachers: A reaction. *Educational Psychologist, 31*, 23–28.

Elkind, D. (1999). Educational research and the science of education. *Educational Psychology Review, 11*, 271–287.

Good, T. L., & Nichols, S. L. (2001). Expectancy effects in the classroom: A special focus on improving the reading performance of minority students in first-grade classrooms. *Educational Psychologist, 36*, 113–126.

Greeno, J. G. (1997). On claims that answer the wrong questions. *Educational Researcher, 26*(1), 5–17.

Grinder, R. E. (1989). Educational psychology: The master science. In M. C. Wittrock & F. Farley (Eds.), *The future of educational psychology: The challenges and opportunities* (pp. 3–18). Hillsdale, NJ: Lawrence Erlbaum Associates, Inc.

Guba, E. G., & Lincoln, Y. S. (1994). Competing paradigms in qualitative research. In N. K. Denzin & Y. S. Lincoln (Eds.), *Handbook of qualitative research* (pp. 105–117). Thousand Oaks, CA: Sage.

Hilgard, E. R. (1996). History of educational psychology. In D. C. Berliner & R. C. Calfee (Eds.), *Handbook of educational psychology* (pp. 990–1004). New York: Macmillan.

Hulme, C., & MacKenzie, S. (1992). *Working memory and severe learning disabilities*. Hillsdale, NJ: Lawrence Erlbaum Associates, Inc.

Klausmeier, H. J. (1988). The future of educational psychology and the content of the graduate program in educational psychology. *Educational Psychologist, 23*, 203–219.

Levin, J. R. (1994). Crafting educational intervention research that's both credible and creditable. *Educational Psychology Review, 6*, 231–243.

Levin, J. R., & O'Donnell, A. M. (1999). What to do about educational research's credibility gaps? *Issues in Education: Contributions From Educational Psychology, 5*, 177–229.

Logie, R. H. (1994). The seven ages of working memory. In J. R. E. Richardson, R. W. Engle, L. Hasher, R. H. Logie, E. R. Stoftzfus, & R. T. Zacks (Eds.), *Working memory and human cognition* (pp. 31–65). New York: Oxford University Press.

Mayer, R. E. (1992). Cognition and instruction: Their historic meeting within educational psychology. *Journal of Educational Psychology, 84*, 405–412.

Mayer, R. E. (2001). What good is educational psychology? The case of cognition and instruction. *Educational Psychologist, 36*, 83–88.

McCaslin, M., & Hickey, D. T. (2001). Educational Psychology, social constructivism, and educational practice: A case of emergent identity. *Educational Psychologist, 36*, 133–140.

Pintrich, P. R. (1994). Continuities and discontinuities: Future directions for research in educational psychology. *Educational Psychologist, 29*, 137–148.

Rothstein, R. (2000). Toward a composite index of school performance. *Elementary School Journal, 100*, 409–441.

Ruediger, W. C., & Strayer, G. D. (1910). The qualities of merit in teachers. *Journal of Educational Psychology, 1*, 272–278.

Scheurman, G., Heeringa, K., Rocklin, T. R., & Lohman, D. F. (1993). Educational psychology: A view from within the discipline. *Educational Psychologist, 28*, 97–115.

Slavin, R. E. (1996). Research on cooperative learning and achievement: What we know, what we need to know. *Contemporary Educational Psychology, 21*, 43–69.

Smith, M. C., Locke, S. G., Boissee, S. J., Gallagher, P. A., Krengel, L. E., Kuczek, J. E., McFarland, J. E., Rapoo, B., & Wertheim, C. (1998). Productivity of educational psychologists in educational psychology journals, 1991–1996. *Contemporary Educational Psychology, 23*, 171–181.

Thorndike, E. L. (1903). *Educational psychology*. New York: Teachers College Press.

Thorndike. E. L. (1910). The contribution of psychology to education. *Journal of Educational Psychology, 1*, 5–12.

Torrance, M., & Jeffrey, G. C. (Eds.). (1999). *The cognitive demands of writing: Processing capacity and working memory effects in text production*. Amsterdam: Amsterdam University Press.

Tudge, J. (2000). Theory, method, and analysis in research on the relations between peer collaboration and cognitive development. *Journal of Experimental Education, 69*, 98–112.

Tweney, R. D., & Budzynski, C. A. (2000). The scientific status of American psychology in 1910. *American Psychologist, 55*, 1014–1017.

Walberg, H. J., & Haertel, G. D. (1992). Educational psychology's first century. *Journal of Educational Psychology, 84*, 6–19.

Wittrock, M. C. (1994). An empowering conception of educational psychology. *Educational Psychologist, 27*, 129–141.

Woolfolk Hoy, A. E. (1996, August). *Appreciated, appropriated, and abandoned*. Division 15 Presidential address at the Annual Meeting of the American Psychological Association, Toronto, Canada.

Zimmerman, B. J., Bonner, S., & Kovak, R. (1996). *Developing self-regulated learners: Beyond achievement to self-efficacy*. Washington, DC: American Psychological Association.

EDUCATIONAL PSYCHOLOGIST, 36(2), 83–88

What Good is Educational Psychology? The Case of Cognition and Instruction

Richard E. Mayer
Department of Psychology
University of California at Santa Barbara

Research on cognition and instruction has made considerable progress in recent years, in terms of contributions both to cognitive theory and to educational practice. Two important contributions are psychologies of subject matter, which specify how people learn school subjects such as reading and mathematics, and teaching of cognitive strategies, which fosters improvements in how students learn and think. In short, the thesis of this essay is that psychology and education are good for one another. When it comes to the role of psychology in education, there is nothing as beneficial to practice as a good theory. When it comes to the role of education in psychology, there is nothing as beneficial to theory as a good practical problem. Although much has been accomplished, the promise of educational psychology in the 21st century rests in the development of an educationally relevant science of how people learn.

It is not easy being an educational psychologist these days. To our colleagues in psychology, we are too educational, a disparaging label reflecting our interest in studying educationally relevant problems rather than contrived laboratory tasks. To our colleagues in education, we are too psychological, a disparaging label reflecting our interest in basing educational practice on scientific research methods and theories rather than relying on popular opinion and doctrine. We disturb psychology by failing to accept contrived artificial laboratory research as the ending-point for psychological research. We disturb education by failing to accept good intentions, expert opinions, and doctrine-based claims as the rationale for educational practices. Yet, it is precisely the juxtaposition of these two criticisms that create the unique potential of educational psychology to advance both psychological theory and educational practice. Educational psychology refuses to turn its back on the study of practical educational problems as a source of rich research questions, and educational psychology refuses to turn its back on the role of scientific research methods and theory in answering educational questions.

THE MUTUAL DEPENDENCE OF PSYCHOLOGY AND EDUCATION

The pages of educational research periodicals have been filled with obituaries cheering the death—or at least the diminished strength—of psychology as a force in education (see Levin & O'Donnell, 1999; Mayer, 1993). To some in the educational research community, psychology has become an irrelevant and troublesome irritation. My goal in this article is to provide examples showing that educational psychology—far from being dead or irrelevant—is a vibrant field that has been experiencing unprecedented success in understanding educational issues. It is ironic, and for me, frustrating, that at a time when educational psychology has matured to the point where its promise for contributing to both education and psychology has never been greater, this is the time that it is in jeopardy of being rejected by both fields. Now that psychologists and educators finally have something worthwhile to talk about, it would be unfortunate for both fields if the conversation was closed.

What Does Education Have to Offer Psychology?

Psychology is a field that has been amazingly successful in studying important human issues within highly artificial, perhaps sterile, environments. The result is the development of research-based theories that are so limited that they are widely recognized as trivial. By the 1950s, the grand theories of learning had died because of their inability to account for learning beyond rats running mazes and pigeons pecking keys. By the 1970s, cognitive psychology, with all of its precisely measured reaction times down to the millisecond, was about to die of its own irrelevance (Neisser, 1976). What

Requests for reprints should be sent to Richard E. Mayer, Department of Psychology, University of California at Santa Barbara, CA 93106. E-mail: mayer@psych.ucsb.edu saved cognitive psychology from its demise was a shift in focus to realistic situations, including educational ones (Mayer, 1992, 1996, 2001). Today, in some research centers, educational and cognitive psychology appear to be merging.

What cognitive psychology needs is the challenge of explaining learning and cognition in realistic situations. To develop theories of learning and cognition that are relevant, psychologists need to examine realistic learning situations. Educational venues offer exactly what cognitive psychology needs: questions about how people learn to read, to comprehend what they read, to write, to compute, to solve mathematics problems, to think scientifically, to think historically, to learn a second language, and so on. Cognitive psychology is enriched by the challenge of developing theories that account for educationally relevant learning and cognition. An example is Chi, Bassok, Lewis, Reimann, and Glaser's (1989) research on how successful and unsuccessful problem solvers study worked-out examples in science textbooks—research that contributes to cognitive theories of analogical reasoning as well as educational practice in science teaching.

What Does Psychology Have to Offer Education?

Education is a field facing monumental practical problems that are often addressed through well-intended fads, expert opinions, and doctrine-based agendas (Levin & O'Donnell, 1999). The result is educational practice that has advanced very little over the last century and still is rarely based on proven instructional techniques. Yet, there is no more important societal task than the education of youth.

What education needs is a set of scientifically valid methods of instruction based on research evidence and tested theory. Help in meeting this need is precisely what psychology has to offer. The scientifically sound research methods of psychology constitute one of the greatest inventions of the 20th century and hold great promise for improving educational practice. Instead of being embarrassed by a commitment to examine educational issues using scientific research methods, educational psychologists should be proud to be able to extend the domain of science into education. Research-based psychological theory can help guide the design of instructional methods and materials.

In short, psychology needs something real to study, and education provides it; education needs a scientific methodology for addressing its problems, and psychology provides it. It is a match made in heaven that has had a somewhat difficult history here on earth. As Mayer (1992) showed, the relation between psychology and education has moved through three phases in the 20th century: (a) a one-way street from psychology to education in which psychology was supposed to develop theories of learning and education was supposed to apply them, (b) a dead-end street for psychology and education in which psychology focused on noneducational issues and education focused mainly on practical issues, and (c) a two-way street between psychology and education in which both disciplines work together for their mutual benefit. Will the two-way street endure as we enter the 21st century or will psychology and education again fall back into their former noncommunicative stance? The thesis of this brief essay is that much is to be gained by continuing the conversation between psychology and education.

WHAT CAN HAPPEN WHEN COGNITION AND INSTRUCTION MEET?

What can happen when psychology and education meet? In this section, I briefly summarize some of the productive results of the collaboration between cognitive psychologists—who aim to understand how people learn—and educators—who aim to understand how to help people learn. Two important contributions of this collaboration between cognition and instruction are the development of psychologies of subject matter, and the teaching of cognitive strategies.

Psychologies of Subject Matter

One of the most productive accomplishments of educational psychology has been the development of psychologies of subject matter (Bruer, 1993; Mayer, 1999; Shulman & Quinlan, 1996). Psychologies of subject matter concern learning and instruction within specific school subjects such as reading, writing, mathematics, science, and history. Instead of examining how people learn in general, psychologies of subject matter examine topics such as how people learn to read, learn to write, learn to think mathematically, learn to think scientifically, and learn to think historically.

One of psychology's original goals—throughout the first half of the 20th century—was the development of a single all-encompassing general theory of learning (Mayer, 2001). In its search for the one true theory of learning, psychology generated several of them ranging from Thorndike's connectionism to Hull's mathematical learning theory to Skinner's behaviorism to Gestalt theory. By midcentury, it had become clear that psychology's search for a general theory of learning was a failure, and eventually the grand theories of learning melted away. Education offered the challenge of understanding how people learn in real school content areas; having failed to establish general theories based on contrived laboratory learning tasks, psychology finally accepted the offer. In short, education rescued psychology from its fruitless search for a general theory of learning. In place of educationally irrelevant general theories, educational psychologists began to develop specific theories tailored to specific subject areas.

In this section, I provide brief examples of the contributions of educational psychology in reading, mathematics, and history.

Psychology of learning to read. What does a child need to know to be able to read? Researchers have shown that one important prerequisite cognitive skill is phonological awareness (or phonemic awareness): awareness that words can be broken down into sound units and that sound units can be combined to form words. For example, phonological awareness involves being able to discriminate the sounds of each of the three letters in the spoken word, "cat;" and being able to produce and blend the sounds of /c/ and /a/ and /t/ to say "cat." Common tests for phonological awareness include being able to (a) tell if two words rhyme (e.g., "cat" and "hat"), (b) recite a list of words (e.g., "hat, fir, led"), (c) tap out the number of sounds in a word (e.g., giving three taps for "cat"), (d) add a sound to a word (e.g., adding "c" to "at" to get "cat"), (e) delete a sound from a word (e.g., taking away the first sound in "cat" to get "at"), or (f) substitute a sound in a word (e.g., given the spoken word "park," change the last sound to /t/ yielding the word "part").

What is the evidence that phonological awareness is related to being able to learn how to read? First, students who have difficulty in learning to read in elementary school score lower on tests of phonological awareness than students who are good readers (Bradley & Bryant, 1978; Stanovich, 1991). Second, students who lack phonological awareness when they enter elementary school are more likely to fail to become strong readers later in elementary school than are students who enter school with phonological awareness (Bradley & Bryant, 1985; Juel, Griffith, & Gough, 1986; Wagner & Torgesen, 1987).

An important educational implication is that students who enter elementary school without skill in phonological awareness could benefit from phonological awareness training. For example, Bradley and Bryant (1983, 1985, 1991) provided phonological awareness training to 5- and 6-year-olds in 40 10-min sessions spread over 2 years. In one session, a student was shown a picture of a bus and asked to pick out another picture of a word that started with the same sound. In another session, a student was shown four pictures and asked to choose the one that began with a different sound from the others. In yet another session, a student was asked to tell whether two spoken words rhymed. A comparison group received 40 10-min lessons involving the same words, but the tasks involved things like sorting pictures based on their semantic category.

Does phonological awareness training work? Students in the trained group showed a strong improvement on tests of phonological awareness, whereas the comparison group did not. Importantly, on a reading test administered after the training, the trained group was five times more likely than the comparison group to be able to read words containing two or three sounds. On a standardized reading test given at the end of the school year, five times as many students were classified as readers in the trained group as in the comparison group. These studies demonstrate that targeted instruction in phonological awareness can have a strong effect on a student's ability to learn to read.

In a recent review, Goswami and Bryant (1992) concluded the following: "There can be little doubt that phonological awareness plays an important role in reading .... There is also evidence that successful training in phonological awareness helps children learn to read" (p. 49). By carefully analyzing the specific knowledge needed to become a reader, by carrying out rigorous longitudinal studies, and by conducting well-controlled intervention experiments, researchers have pinpointed a potentially important factor in early reading instruction—namely, phonological awareness. This line of research is a little gem of educational research because it represents a powerful example of how educational psychology can contribute to education and psychology.

Psychology of mathematics learning. What does a student need to know to learn basic arithmetic, such as how to add and subtract single-digit numbers? One concept targeted by researchers is number sense, which includes the concept of the mental line and the ability to use it. Number sense can be tested by asking questions such as, "What number comes after 7?", "Which is closer to 5—6 or 2?", "Which number comes first when you are counting—8, 5, 2, or 6?", and "Which number is bigger—5 or 4?".

What evidence is there that a child's knowledge of the mental number line is related to learning arithmetic? Case and his colleagues developed a test of students' knowledge of the mental number line (Case & Okamoto, 1996; Griffin, Case, & Capodilupo, 1995; Griffin, Case, & Siegler, 1994). When they administered the test to 6-year-old children, they found that most of the children from low socioeconomic status (SES) homes lacked an adequate knowledge of the mental number line, and also most could not solve simple arithmetic problems such as, "2 + 4 = ___." In contrast, most of the high SES children demonstrated adequate knowledge of the mental number line and also most could solve simple arithmetic problems. This line of research suggests that an obstacle to learning basic arithmetic may be that some students enter school without a conception of a mental number line.

Does number line training work? If knowledge of a mental line is a cognitive prerequisite for learning arithmetic, then students who lack this knowledge could benefit from instruction that is specifically targeted at helping them develop it. For example, the "Rightstart" program consists of 40 half-hour sessions in which students learn how to use a mental number line by playing various games (Griffin & Case, 1996; Griffin et al., 1994, 1995). The games give students experience in comparing two dice to see which number is higher, moving a token along a number-line path based on the number on the die, moving a token backwards along a number-line path for a certain number of steps, and so on.

Low SES first graders who received the training showed large improvements on tests of number-line knowledge, whereas a comparison group that received traditional mathematics instruction did not. More importantly, on an arithmetic test given at the end of the year, twice as many of the trained students mastered basic arithmetic as did students in the comparison group. Griffin and Case (1996) concluded that "a surprising proportion of children from low-income homes in North American families—at least 50% in our samples—do not arrive in school with the central conceptual structure in place that is necessary for success in first grade mathematics" (p. 102). This knowledge deficiency can be remedied through careful, focused instructional activities. Number-line training is an important example of how educational psychology can contribute to education and psychology. It is another little gem in the crown of educational psychology.

Psychology of history learning. As a final example, let's consider the knowledge that is needed for upper-elementary school students to understand their history textbooks. Research on reading comprehension has demonstrated that people understand a passage by relating the presented material to their relevant prior knowledge. If a student lacks relevant prior knowledge, the student will have difficulty in understanding a textbook passage.

For example, Beck, McKeown, Sinatra, and Loxterman (1991) asked fourth and fifth graders to read a U.S. history passage about the French and Indian War that began with the following sentence: "In 1763, Britain and the colonies ended a 7-year war with the French and Indians." Based on interviews with students, McKeown and Beck (1990) determined that most students lacked useful background knowledge such as the idea that Britain and France both wanted the same piece of land in North America, that the conflict over this land resulted in a 7-year war called the French and Indian War, and that the colonies belonged to Britain and so they sided with Britain, whereas the Indians sided with France.

Beck et al. (1991) rewrote the passage so that it would help students use appropriate prior knowledge, including their knowledge that two people wanting the same object can lead to conflict. For example, the first sentence was expanded to include the following:

> About 250 years ago, Britain and France both claimed to own some of the same land here in North America … . In 1756, Britain and France went to war to see who would get control of the land. Because the 13 American colonies belonged to Britain, the colonists fought on the same side as Britain. Many Indians fought on the same side as France. (p. 257)

In this way, Beck et al. (1991) helped students prime their "conflict schema"—their prior knowledge that conflicts occur when two people both want to possess the same object. Activating this schema is intended to help students organize the material in a meaningful way.

Does schema activation help students learn? Students who read a revised version of the textbook passage scored more than 50% higher on an essay test than did students who read the original version of the passage (Beck et al., 1991). These results show that a prerequisite to meaningful learning of history is that students possess and activate appropriate prior knowledge. This line of research on schema activation is another example of the contribution of educational psychology to education and psychology. It is yet another little gem of educational psychology research.

Teaching of Cognitive Strategies

Another important development in educational psychology is the teaching of cognitive strategies (Pressley & Woloshyn, 1995; Weinstein & Mayer, 1986). Cognitive strategies are cognitive processes that the learner intentionally performs to influence learning and cognition. Examples include basic processes such as using a rehearsal strategy to memorize a list and metacognitive strategies such as recognizing whether one comprehends a passage.

In this section, I briefly summarize research on teaching of strategies for learning lists, strategies for comprehension of text, and strategies for solving problems.

List learning strategies. Belmont and Butterfield (1971) found that special-education students performed more poorly on learning a list of six letters than did regular-education students. In addition, the special-education students generally did not spontaneously engage in any rehearsal strategies (such as repeating the list aloud), whereas the regular-education students often did rehearse. However, when special education students were explicitly taught to rehearse, by stating the list aloud, their performance on remembering lists increased to the level of the regular-education students.

Reading comprehension strategies. Brown and Palinscar (1989; Palinscar & Brown, 1984) showed that it is possible to teach seventh graders how to use reading comprehension strategies such as questioning, in which the student creates an appropriate question for a passage; clarifying, in which a student detects and corrects any potential comprehension difficulties such as definitions of unfamiliar words; summarizing, in which a student produces a concise summary for a passage; and predicting, in which a student suggests what will come next in subsequent text. In some studies, students who were given focused and sustained training in these strategies showed substantial gains in their reading comprehension performance, whereas comparison students who received conventional instruction did not.

Problem-solving strategies. Covington, Crutchfield, Davies, and Olton (1974) developed a program intended to teach elementary school students how to generate and test hypotheses within the context of detective stories. Students who received training over an extended period of time were better able to solve detective-like problems than were equivalent students who had not received training (Mansfield, Busse, & Krepelka, 1978; Olton & Crutchfield, 1969).

In each case, students learned specific learning strategies that improved their performance on new tasks. Research on teaching of cognitive strategies represents a landmark contribution of educational psychology. For example, Pressley and Woloshyn (1995) argued that "cognitive strategies … represent the most important instructional advance of the past 15 years" (p. iii). Armed with a solid research base, it is now possible to improve how students learn and think, by helping them develop and use appropriate cognitive strategies.

The work I highlighted represents only a few examples of educational psychology's contributions to education and psychology. Furthermore, psychologies of subject matter and teaching of cognitive strategies represent just two fruitful areas of contribution. Other important areas of contribution include the development of new conceptions of intellectual ability, new ways of assessing learning outcomes, and new ways of designing computer-based (or Web-based) instruction. Research on cognitive strategies contributes to cognitive theories of learning by pinpointing the knowledge that learners build, and contributes to educational practice by specifying the knowledge that students need for various tasks.

Development of an Educationally Relevant Science

Perhaps the most enduring outcome of the meeting of cognition and instruction is the development of educationally relevant theories of learning and cognition (Bransford, Brown, & Cocking, 1999; Bruer, 1993; Lambert & McCombs, 1998; Mayer, 1999). The development of an educationally relevant science fulfills the century-old dream of the world's first educational psychologist, E. L. Thorndike, in which teachers "direct their choices of methods by the results of scientific investigation rather than general opinion" (Thorndike, 1906, p. 257). After 100 years of progress, educational psychology faces the new century with research methods and theories that have the potential for improving both educational practice and psychological theory (Mayer, in press).

Our challenge is to get psychologists and educators to work together to solve the dilemmas of education. A potentially useful solution is to encourage teachers to skillfully teach learners cognitive strategies in specific subject areas and to encourage psychologists to skillfully study educationally relevant problems.

In short, psychology and education are good for one another. When it comes to the role of psychology in education, my argument is that there is nothing as beneficial to practice as a good theory. When it comes to the role of education in psychology, my argument is that there is nothing as beneficial to theory as a good practical problem. Although much has been accomplished, the promise of educational psychology remains great in the new century.

REFERENCES

Beck, I. L., McKeown, M. G., Sinatra, G. M., & Loxterman, J. A. (1991). Revising social studies text from a text-processing perspective: Evidence for improved comprehensibility. *Reading Research Quarterly, 26*, 251–276.

Belmont, J. M., & Butterfield, E. C. (1971). Learning strategies as determinants of memory deficiencies. *Cognitive Psychology, 2*, 411–420.

Bradley, L., & Bryant, P. (1978). Difficulties in auditory organization as a possible cause of reading backwardness. *Nature, 271*, 746–747.

Bradley, L., & Bryant, P. (1983). Categorizing sounds and learning to read: A causal connection. *Nature, 301*, 419–421.

Bradley, L., & Bryant, P. (1985). *Rhyme and reason in reading and spelling*. Ann Arbor: University of Michigan Press.

Bradley, L., & Bryant, P. (1991). Phonological skills before and after learning to read. In S. A. Brady & D. P. Shankweiler (Eds.), *Phonological processes in literacy* (pp. 37–45). Hillsdale, NJ: Lawrence Erlbaum Associates, Inc.

Bransford, J. D., Brown, A. L., & Cocking, R. R. (Eds.). (1999). *How people learn*. Washington, DC: National Academy Press.

Brown, A. L., & Palinscar, A. S. (1989). Guided, cooperative learning and individual knowledge acquisition. In L. B. Resnick (Ed.), *Knowing, learning, and instruction* (pp. 393–451). Hillsdale, NJ: Lawrence Erlbaum Associates, Inc.

Bruer, J. T. (1993). *Schools for thought*. Cambridge, MA: MIT Press.

Case, R., & Okamoto, Y. (1996). The role of central conceptual structures in the development of children's thought. *Monographs of the Society for Research in Child Development, 61*, 246.

Chi, M. T. H., Bassok, M., Lewis, M. W., Reimann, P., & Glaser, R. (1989). Self-explanations: How students study and use examples in learning to solve problems. *Cognitive Science, 13*, 66–71.

Covington, M. V., Crutchfield, R. S., Davies, L. B., & Olton, R. M. (1974). *The productive thinking program*. Columbus, OH: Merrill.

Goswami, U., & Bryant, P. (1992). Rhyme, analogy, and children's reading. In P. B. Gough, L. C. Ehri, & R. Treiman (Eds.), *Reading acquisition* (pp. 49–63). Hillsdale, NJ: Lawrence Erlbaum Associates, Inc.

Griffin, S., & Case, R. (1996). Evaluating the breadth and depth of training effects when central conceptual structures are taught. *Monographs of the Society for Research in Child Development, 61*, 83–102.

Griffin, S. A., Case, R., & Capodilupo, S. (1995). Teaching for understanding: The importance of central conceptual structures in the elementary school mathematics curriculum. In A. McKeough, J. Lupart, & A. Marini (Eds.), *Teaching for transfer: Fostering generalization in learning* (pp. 123–151). Hillsdale, NJ: Lawrence Erlbaum Associates, Inc.

Griffin, S. A., Case, R., & Siegler, R. S. (1994). Rightstart: Providing the central conceptual prerequisites for first formal learning of arithmetic to students at risk for school failure. In K. McGilly (Ed.), *Classroom lessons: Integrating cognitive theory and classroom practice* (pp. 25–49). Cambridge, MA: MIT Press.

Juel, C., Griffith, P. L., & Gough, P. B. (1986). Acquisition of literacy: A longitudinal study of children in first and second grade. *Journal of Educational Psychology, 78,* 243–255.

Lambert, N. M., & McCombs, B. L. (1998). *How students learn.* Washington, DC: American Psychological Association.

Levin, J. R., & O'Donnell, A. (1999). What to do about educational research's credibility gaps? *Issues in Education, 5,* 177–229.

Mansfield, R. S., Busse, T. V., & Krepelka, E. J. (1978). The effectiveness of creativity training. *Review of Educational Research, 48,* 517–536.

Mayer, R. E. (1992). Cognition and instruction: On their historic meeting within educational psychology. *Journal of Educational Psychology, 84,* 405–412.

Mayer, R. E. (1993). Outmoded conceptions of educational research. *Educational Researcher, 22*(9), 6.

Mayer, R. E. (1996). Learners as information processors: Legacies and limitations of educational psychology's second metaphor. *Educational Psychologist, 31,* 151–161.

Mayer, R. E. (1999). *The promise of educational psychology.* Upper Saddle River, NJ: Prentice Hall.

Mayer, R. E. (2001). Changing conceptions of learning: A century of progress in the scientific study of education. In L. Corno (Ed.), *Yearbook of the National Society for the Study of Education* (pp. 34–75). Chicago: University of Chicago Press.

Mayer, R. E. (in press). E. L. Thorndike's enduring contributions to educational psychology. In B. J. Zimmerman and D. H. Schunk (Eds.), *Educational psychology: A century of contributions.* Mahwah, NJ: Lawrence Erlbaum Associates, Inc.

McKeown, M. G., & Beck, I. L. (1990). The assessment and characterization of young learners' knowledge of a topic in history. *American Educational Research Journal, 27,* 688–726.

Neisser, U. (1976). *Cognition and reality.* San Francisco: Freeman.

Olton, R. M., & Crutchfield, R. S. (1969). Developing the skills of productive thinking. In P. Mussen, J. Langer, & M. V. Covington (Eds.), *Trends and issues in developmental psychology* (pp. 68–91). New York: Holt, Rinehart & Winston.

Palinscar, A. S., & Brown, A. L. (1984). Reciprocal teaching of comprehension-fostering and monitoring strategies. *Cognition and Instruction, 1,* 117–175.

Pressley, M., & Woloshyn, V. (1995). *Cognitive strategy instruction that really improves children's academic performance* (2nd ed.). Cambridge, MA: Brookline.

Shulman, L. S., & Quinlan, S. S. (1996). The comparative psychology of school subjects. In D. C. Berliner & R. C. Calfee (Eds.), *Handbook of educational psychology* (pp. 399–422). New York: Macmillan.

Stanovich, K. E. (1991). Discrepancy definitions of reading disability: Has intelligence led us astray? *Reading Research Quarterly, 26,* 7–26.

Thorndike, E. L. (1906). *The principles of teaching based on psychology.* Syracuse, NY: Mason-Henry Press.

Wagner, R. K., & Torgesen, J. K. (1987). The nature of phonological processing and its causal role in the acquisition of reading skills. *Psychological Bulletin, 101,* 192–212.

Weinstein, C. E., & Mayer, R. E. (1986). The teaching of learning strategies. In M. C. Wittrock (Ed.), *Handbook of research on teaching* (3rd ed., pp. 315–327). New York: Macmillan.

EDUCATIONAL PSYCHOLOGIST, *36*(2), 89–101

Classroom Applications of Research on Self-Regulated Learning

Scott G. Paris
Department of Psychology
University of Michigan

Alison H. Paris
Combined Program in Education and Psychology
University of Michigan

This article describes how self-regulated learning (SRL) has become a popular topic in research in educational psychology and how the research has been translated into classroom practices. Research during the past 30 years on students' learning and achievement has progressively included emphases on cognitive strategies, metacognition, motivation, task engagement, and social supports in classrooms. SRL emerged as a construct that encompassed these various aspects of academic learning and provided more holistic views of the skills, knowledge, and motivation that students acquire. The complexity of SRL has been appealing to educational researchers who seek to provide effective interventions in schools that benefit teachers and students directly. Examples of SRL in classrooms are provided for three areas of research: strategies for reading and writing, cognitive engagement in tasks, and self-assessment. The pedagogical principles and underlying research are discussed for each area. Whether SRL is viewed as a set of skills that can be taught explicitly or as developmental processes of self-regulation that emerge from experience, teachers can provide information and opportunities to students of all ages that will help them become strategic, motivated, and independent learners.

A primary purpose of this special issue is to document the contributions of research in educational psychology to classroom practices that promote teaching and learning. Educational psychology, perhaps more than many areas in academic psychology, seeks to bridge theory and practice because the improvement of education is an underlying goal of most researchers. Thus, the question "What has educational psychology done for you lately?" is more than rhetorical. It is a challenge to demonstrate the value and the pragmatic outcomes of research for teachers, policymakers, and others involved in enhancing educational practices. Some may suggest that this endeavor is symptomatic of a new era when political and economic pressures for accountability require academics to justify and publicize their accomplishments. Others may counter that we are "preaching to the choir" with this argument appearing in a specialized scholarly journal. Still others might be proud to illustrate the positive impact of research on educational practice. We belong to the latter camp of enthusiastic optimists who regard the past 30 years of research in educational psychology as an exciting proliferation of useful ideas for teachers and students.

Our specific focus in this article is self-regulated learning, a topic that has garnered a great deal of interest among academic researchers and practicing educators because it is a worthy objective for students of all ages in all disciplines. Self-regulated learning (SRL), as the three words imply, emphasizes autonomy and control by the individual who monitors, directs, and regulates actions toward goals of information acquisition, expanding expertise, and self-improvement. Zimmerman (2000) said that self-regulation, "… refers to self-generated thoughts, feelings, and actions that are planned and cyclically adapted to the attainment of personal goals" (p.14). The broad and indefinite scope of SRL appeals to researchers and educators who seek to understand how students become adept and independent in their educational pursuits. For example, students who daydream, forget assignments, and rarely complete their work, display little SRL. In contrast, students who ask questions, take notes, and allocate their time and resources judiciously are in charge of

Requests for reprints should be sent to Scott G. Paris, Department of Psychology, University of Michigan, 2008 East Hall, 525 East University Avenue, Ann Arbor, MI 48109. E-mail: sparis@umich.edu their own learning. We briefly note some historical and conceptual approaches to SRL and then provide examples of classroom practices that enhance SRL. Specifically, we describe how SRL is manifested in students' strategic reading and writing, task engagement, and self-assessment.

HISTORICAL TRENDS IN RESEARCH ON SELF-REGULATED LEARNING

The *Educational Psychologist* has promoted attention to SRL with a series of special issues over the years. For example, there were special issues devoted to academic studying (Levin & Pressley, 1986), metacognition (Paris, 1987), SRL theories (Zimmerman, 1990), motivational influences on education (Brophy, 1999), and social influences on school adjustment (Wentzel & Berndt, 1999). In addition, since 1990 there have been more than 30 articles published in the *Educational Psychologist* on topics directly related to SRL. The wide range of topics has included phenomenological aspects of SRL (McCombs & Marzano, 1990), children's social regulation (Patrick, 1997), family influences on self-regulation (Grolnick, Kurowski, & Gurland, 1999), social and cultural influences on SRL (Boekaerts, 1998; Pressley, 1995), monitoring reading (Pressley & Ghatala, 1990), personal cognitive development (Ferrari & Mahalingam, 1998), and specific influences of situation and domain knowledge on SRL (Alexander, 1995). The variety of topics relevant to SRL illustrates how it is interwoven with many aspects of education and development (Paris & Newman, 1990; Pintrich & DeGroot, 1990).

Because SRL is relevant to so many aspects of learning and control, diverse theoretical perspectives have been proposed as useful for examining SRL. These include theories based on Piaget's constructivist theory, Vygotsky's sociocultural theory, social learning theories, and information-processing theories. Zimmerman and Schunk (1989, 2001) highlighted these different approaches by asking authors in their volumes to examine SRL from distinctive theoretical stances (even though a mix of eclecticism is evident in most research). For example, it is commonly accepted now that children construct beliefs, concepts, and naïve theories about the psychological world, especially their own views of epistemology. It is equally accepted that adults and peers shape those emerging theories through sociocognitive processes of guided participation, scaffolded assistance, and apprenticeship. Goals that guide plans and behavior, volition to enact them, and feelings of self-efficacy that follow task completion are also accepted as motivational accompaniments of SRL (Pintrich, 2000; Schunk & Ertmer, 2000). The theoretical lineage of these ideas is less important to teachers than the practical applications of the concepts. We think SRL theories that emphasize how other people can help children learn tactics to regulate their own behavior and learning have had the most direct application to classrooms because they have both theoretical and practical foundations.

Although there are numerous conceptual approaches to research on SRL, there is a need to identify explicitly the practical applications of SRL to classrooms. It seems to us that there are at least two reasons for this. First, there are increasing historical pressures to synthesize findings in educational psychology and link research with practice. Second, there have been historical changes in the practical relevance of research in educational psychology so that the benefits of interventions are made available to more students with methods that teachers can adapt and use in their classrooms. These historical changes are evident in research on cognitive strategies and instruction that led to the popularity of SRL. We briefly trace the historical convergence of these topics on SRL.

The Nature of Strategies

Consider the changes in research on strategies during the early years of the "cognitive revolution" in educational psychology. First, the grain size has increased. Cognitive research in the 1970s still employed the "magnifying glass" approach of earlier behavioral research whereby aspects of thinking were isolated, examined, and deconstructed into components, perhaps to be reassembled later in models or recommendations. Early studies examined specific strategies such as summarizing text, whereas later research examined the diverse ways that readers respond to text. Research in the 1970s investigated who used which strategies, however, by the 1980s, researchers began experimental implementations of various strategy conditions. In the 1990s, strategy research progressed to studies of classroom programs of strategy intervention.

Second, the variety and relevance of strategies has increased. Weinstein and Mayer (1986) summarized the major categories of general learning strategies as rehearsal strategies, elaboration strategies, organizational strategies, comprehension monitoring strategies, and affective strategies. Research in the 1970s demonstrated that students who were handicapped by youth, inexperience, or lack of understanding failed to use these kinds of strategies as effectively as older and more expert students. Later studies considered a broader range of tactics that students can marshal in school for specific subjects and purposes.

Third, ecological validity has increased. In the last 20 years, research on learning strategies has been conducted in classrooms, with more attention given to ecological and functional orientations. Researchers examined the kinds of strategies that students use as they read and write or as they solve mathematical and scientific problems. There has also been more attention to the methods and materials that teachers use to promote strategic learning.

Fourth, the social collaboration and scaffolding required to use those strategies were implemented in classrooms. In the 1990s, there were detailed studies of the social and motivational conditions that support students' use of effective strategies. Teachers have used pair-share activities, reciprocal teaching (Palincsar & Brown, 1984), and collaborative learning to allow children to coach each other to monitor and improve their own learning. Thus, learning strategies have become important cognitive tools for teachers to model, explain, and foster in their students throughout the curriculum.

The Nature of Instruction

During the past 30 years, the nature of instruction has changed dramatically. Early "training" studies emphasized didactic methods, whereas recent approaches emphasize reflective and scaffolded instruction. Early strategy training studies were conducted in laboratory experiments rather than in classrooms. Ann Brown (1978) characterized these studies as "blind training" and later studies as "informed" because the instructional conditions became more cognitive and explanatory. Research in the 1980s simultaneously increased the grain size of the issues and situated strategy research in classrooms in four distinct ways. First, metacognition was added to the research on strategies so that training included explanations about how strategies operate and why they are useful rather than simple directions to use them. In retrospect, it seems incredibly short-sighted that researchers would not routinely explain how, why, and when strategies are effective. However, the emphasis was on experimental control and rigor, and so children were usually told what to do rather than provided with more explanatory rationales for their actions. Fuller disclosure led to better learning. Explicit instruction on declarative, procedural, and conditional knowledge that underlies effective strategic learning was the hallmark of strategy training in the 1980s (Paris, Wixson, & Palincsar, 1986; Pressley, Harris, & Marks, 1992).

Second, motivation and emotion were added to cognitive dimensions of learning. Consequently, training students to use strategies for learning also entailed making the strategies fun and functional. In fact, the old componential and additive models of learning were threatened by these new classroom interventions that wove fun and information together inextricably. Third, strategies were situated in specific disciplines, beginning with reading in the 1970s and extending to mathematics, science, and social studies as researchers recognized that each discipline afforded different frameworks for organizing knowledge (Alexander, 1995). Fourth, strategy research moved from the laboratory into schools because researchers wanted to test whether students could be taught to use effective strategies in their regular curricula. The interplay of all four factors are evident in the instructional conversations designed to enhance students' awareness of strategies and problem-solving techniques. Instruction is not telling students what to do or what strategies should be applied. Rather cognitive instruction involves students in reflective discourses about thinking with multiple opportunities to talk about the task and how to solve it. Explanations, guided inquiry, scaffolded support, reciprocal teaching, and collaborative learning all foster discourse among students and teachers about how to use strategies appropriately and to learn effectively.

The historical convergence of research on strategies, awareness, and control necessary for SRL is evident in this brief review. More generally, the complexity of learning was recognized in the interactions among knowledge, skills, and dispositions for all disciplines. It is especially useful for students to be reflective and metacognitive at three times: during initial learning, while troubleshooting, and while teaching others to use strategies (Paris, Lipson, & Wixson, 1983). SRL depends on motivation and control as well. Students need to be motivated to exert effort, to persist in the face of difficulty, to set attainable yet challenging goals, and to feel self-efficacy with their own accomplishments. They need the volitional control to avoid distractions and stay on track (Corno, 1993). They also benefit from using emotion control, such as reassuring self-speech, to limit anxiety about task difficulty (Kuhl, 1984). It is the fusing of skill and will (and dare we add "thrill?") to emphasize that cognition, motivation, and affect are all involved in SRL. Similar emphases are apparent in educational movements called "learning to learn," "higher order thinking," "mindful learning," "reflective teaching and learning," "autonomous learning," and "flow experiences" that all emphasize the core principles of SRL.

SRL researchers did not discover or invent these processes of learning and SRL holds no privilege or dominion over the study of learning. New terms and emphases will emerge in future studies. What is important to understand, however, are the historical changes that have percolated throughout educational psychology the past 30 years that have made SRL popular as a contemporary topic in research and a focus in classroom practices. Educational psychologists learned quickly that teaching students to use strategies appropriately involved metacognition, motivation, domain-specific knowledge, and features of the classroom tasks. These multiple and interactive forces are the expanded focus of SRL.

The historical changes have moved research from small grain to large grain foci in the study of learning to study how students plan, monitor, and revise their actions as they engage the curriculum. The shift has also been from decontextualized laboratory research to discipline-based applications so that SRL research has illuminated specific strategies and motivations that enhance achievement in specific subject areas. Research has also moved beyond training based on following directions to teaching based on cognitive discussions. Finally, there has been a shift from highly controlled research in artificial settings that might be translated into educational practice to less controlled research that is situated in schools and embodies effective practices within the implementation and research. In the following sections we identify specific examples of SRL in classrooms and the kinds of research on which it is built.

STRATEGIC READING AND WRITING

Much of the early research on cognitive strategies in the 1960s and 1970s focused on children's memory development and it was a short jump for researchers to study the kinds of strategies children use as they read and write. For example, the literacy strategies used by school-age children can be described according to the time at which they use them (e.g., preliteracy, during literacy, or postliteracy experience). Before children begin to read, it is useful to preview texts and to establish a purpose for reading. It may also be useful to make inferences from the text source, titles, pictures, and skimming of information before one begins to read. However, these strategies are difficult for many children throughout elementary school (Paris, Wasik, & Turner, 1991). Similar kinds of strategies facilitate writing, however 8- to 12-year-olds are often reluctant to use brainstorming, semantic webs, and peer discussions to guide their initial drafts. Instruction in prewriting and prereading strategies has consistently shown positive benefits for elementary school students (Pressley, Johnson, Symons, McGoldrick, & Kurita, 1989).

One of the key strategies that children learn to use as they read is to make inferences and elaborate the meaning from text. However, without explicit instructions, children often focus on the literal meaning of text rather than transforming it into their own words and ideas (Johnston & Afflerbach, 1985). In addition, children in upper elementary grades have difficulty identifying main ideas and difficulty distinguishing important from unimportant information (Baumann, 1984). The focus on literal meaning and the inability to distinguish main ideas may arise from inappropriate comprehension goals or the lack of appropriate strategies employed while reading. In the same vein, children often fail to monitor and repair their writing when they are engaged in the task. They often do not reread for comprehensibility or use topic sentences and main ideas to organize their writing.

After children finish reading a passage, they often do not look back in texts to check their understanding or make good summaries. For example, Brown and Day (1983) found that fifth and seventh graders, when trying to summarize a passage, tended to recall bits of information in the same sequence as the text, and did not plan their summaries effectively. They often ran out of space on the page before they had completed their summaries. Winograd (1984) found a similar pattern among eighth graders when asked to summarize. Again, there is a parallel with writing strategies. Students who are asked to revise frequently make superficial changes and fail to appreciate the audience's perspective or monitor the comprehensibility of their text. Children who use effective strategies for revising may follow the advice of a peer, may reread their own writing from a different perspective, and are more likely to embellish ideas as they revise.

Literacy Strategies Within an SRL Framework

From these studies of the use of specific strategies, research on strategic reading and writing has changed in two critical ways: (a) by increasing in grain size, and (b) by focusing on the practical applications of strategy instruction in classrooms. First, rather than examining specific strategies such as summarizing or editing, research on reading and writing strategies became embedded in SRL to include a wider variety of strategies as well as broader types of strategies (e.g., executive control strategies). This change was necessitated because of the growing realization that the effective use of literacy strategies depended on awareness of procedural, declarative, and conditional knowledge, as well as motivational attributions and feelings of efficacy. That is, students need to know what actions lead to which outcomes and why it is important to perform and monitor those actions. Feedback is instrumental as well as emotional. Borkowski, Carr, Rellinger, and Pressley (1990) referred to the orchestration of these multiple factors as the "good strategy-user" model. Training children to be more strategic readers and writers thus involved making children aware of potential strategies, helping them to attribute success to good strategies, and helping them to choose and monitor appropriate strategies. As an example of the increased grain size in strategy research, Graham (1997) examined the role of executive control strategies in the revising process of sixth-grade students who struggled with writing. Providing students with support in managing and coordinating their plans and decisions had positive effects on their revising behavior (e.g., increasing the number of nonsurface revisions) and the quality of the text that they produced. Page-Voth and Graham (1999) investigated the role of goal-setting strategies in improving the writing performance of seventh- and eighth-grade students. Students learned strategies that would facilitate goal attainment by helping them to coordinate processes that involved generation, evaluation, and incorporation of target elements into their essays. Students who learned the goal-setting strategy wrote longer papers, included more supporting reasons, and produced qualitatively better essays than students in the control condition.

Second, shifts in the nature of strategy research are evident in the growing number of demonstrations of effective instructional interventions that promote children's strategy use. The more recent classroom-based studies attend to the role of teachers, teaching practices, and materials in mediating children's development of literacy strategies. For example, Palincsar and Brown (1984) taught junior high students to work in pairs as they practiced using reading strategies, a practice called "reciprocal teaching." Paris, Cross, and Lipson (1984) used classroom discussions about strategies to promote understanding among third and fifth graders. Pressley, Almasi, Schuder, Bergman, and Kurita (1994) used "transactional instruction" to promote the use of reading strategies. Englert et al. (1991) embedded cognitive and metacognitive strategy instruction in a writing program for fourth- and fifth-grade students. Instruction included direct explanation of writing strategies and modeled use, daily writing with topics usually selected by students, use of procedural facilitation in the form of think-sheets, peer review and feedback, frequent writing conferences, and publication of student papers. Harris and Graham (1992) taught children a variety of practical strategies for organizing, planning, and revising their compositions. They taught self-instructional tactics to promote self-regulation such as identifying the problem, focusing on the task, applying the strategies, evaluating performance, coping with anxiety and maintaining self-control, self-reinforcement, goal-setting, self-assessment, and self-monitoring. Harris and Graham (1996) stressed the necessity of incorporating SRL components into classroom instruction, arguing that maintenance and generalization of strategy use will suffer if SRL components are neglected. At the heart of this instruction are the following six recursive stages: (a) activating and developing background knowledge, (b) discussion, (c) cognitive modeling, (d) mnemonic memorization, (e) supported performance, and (f) independent performance.

These programs of strategy instruction exemplify several key features of successful interventions. One key is to provide a rich variety of strategies that children can use on academic tasks. Children must know the types of available strategies that lead to understanding and success before they will be able to implement them. Second, as intervention studies have shown, teachers need to share specific strategy information that is required for students to become aware of how, when, and why to apply strategies. A third important principle is the causal attribution of improved performance to the effective application of effort in using the strategy. If students believe that strategy use is the reason for success rather than attributing success to more stable factors (e.g., ability) or less controllable ones (e.g., luck, the teacher), they are more likely to utilize effective strategies in the future. A fourth key is that effective strategies can be learned from peers by engaging students in situations that make strategy use observable and salient, such as during discussion and tutoring. Fifth, academic literacy strategies are part of larger plans for managing one's effort, resources, and emotions; therefore, strategy instruction in literacy may set the stage for transfer of strategy use to other domains, as well as perhaps for a more self-regulated approach to learning in general. Sixth, it is important for strategies to be embedded in daily activities so that teachers and students have opportunities to practice the strategies in authentic activities throughout the curriculum. If the nature of activities and their participation structures implicitly require the use of strategies, students will be more likely to develop thoughtful approaches to learning than if they are limited to situations where strategy use is coerced or directed.

COGNITIVE ENGAGEMENT

Most of the research on SRL has focused on identifying and enhancing the use of effective strategies, mainly as in-the-head features of solo cognition. However, context cannot be ignored. Whether students use self-regulating tactics in school, what kinds of strategies they use, how they are rewarded for their use, and how much effort they expend being regulated and strategic, depends on the tasks and contexts that teachers create for students. Research in the 1990s has used social and ecological perspectives to examine the kinds of instructional activities that support SRL with particular attention on how task demands and constraints of the situation influence students' learning and motivation. This is the bridge from "situated cognition" to "situated motivation" (Paris & Turner, 1994). For example, Blumenfeld and her colleagues explained that variety, diversity, challenge, control, and meaningfulness, as well as the procedural complexity and social organization of the task, affect the use of deep-level learning strategies (Blumenfeld, 1992; Blumenfeld, Mergendoller, & Swarthout, 1987). Conversely, when teachers structure classroom tasks that emphasize peer competition, rote procedures, and behavioral management, students are likely to perceive classroom tasks as busy work, to focus on completing the task, and to engage in the activities in superficial manners (Blumenfeld, Hamilton, Bossert, Wessels, & Meece, 1983; Doyle, 1983).

Cognitive engagement approaches emphasize how features of academic tasks influence the quality of students' learning. Definitions of cognitive engagement vary among researchers, but they include meaningful and thoughtful approaches to tasks. When students are deeply engaged, they go beyond the requirements of the assignment, they exhibit preferences for challenge and risk-taking, and they make psychological investments to master the knowledge and skills (Connell & Wellborn, 1991; Newmann, Wehlage, & Lamborn, 1992; Wehlage, 1989). This perspective assumes that students will only be engaged when the context meets their needs and affords the opportunity to become immersed in the task. This requires that tasks elicit the intrinsic interests of students, permit a sense of ownership, relate to life outside of school, allow for collaboration, communicate high expectations, and offer consistent support for students to meet those expectations (Marks, Doane, & Secada, 1996; Newmann et al., 1992; Wehlage, 1989). Conversely, if classroom instruction offers only superficial or low-level tasks (e.g., rote memorization, worksheets), it is doubtful that students will be required to engage in thoughtful and strategic ways.

Research that has focused on classroom tasks sheds light on the challenge of how teachers can design instructional activities that promote independent, strategic, and effortful learning. For example, Turner (1995) found that first-grade teachers were very different in the amount of independence they allowed in their reading curriculum. Whether teachers regarded themselves as primarily "basal" or "whole language" teachers, some designed classrooms with many open-ended activities. In contrast, Turner (1995) found that other teachers designed their reading tasks with more restrictive opportunities to exercise SRL, tasks that she labeled as "closed," such as filling in worksheets. In open task structures, students had choices about what, where, and when they read. They were able to choose personally meaningful materials that were appropriately difficult and to work with a partner or with groups on authentic projects and research. In contrast, closed tasks limited the opportunities for decision making, controlled the choice of materials and activities, limited the variation in the types of tasks, and encouraged solitary seatwork. In the open-ended environments, Turner (1995) found that students demonstrated more volitional control, used more strategies, and persisted longer in the face of difficulties. Thus, open-ended tasks that promote thoughtful engagement include opportunities for students to make choices, exercise control, set challenging goals, collaborate with others, construct personal meaning, and derive feelings of self-efficacy as a consequence of their engagement with the task (Paris & Turner, 1994).

Connell and Wellborn (1991) emphasized that engagement depends on the extent to which students' needs for competence, autonomy, and relatedness are satisfied. Their focus is on specific contextual factors to meet these needs, which include the provision of structure, autonomy support, and involvement. Behavioral, affective, and cognitive engagement will ensue when the appropriate interaction between the classroom context and the child occurs. Such an ecological approach emphasizes the "fit" between the environment and the child, an approach that is similar to "developmentally appropriate practice" in early childhood education. For example, Stipek, Feiler, Daniels, and Milburn (1995) distinguished between young children in child-centered classrooms and children in teacher-directed classrooms and found that the 4- to 6-year-olds in child-centered classes demonstrated more attitudes and behaviors associated with SRL. Child-centered classrooms encouraged peer interaction and gave children choices about a diverse set of activities and materials that were meaningful to students. In contrast, teacher-directed classrooms focused on basic skills that were not embedded in meaningful activities and were controlled by the teachers. They also used external evaluations and rewards, and they emphasized performance goals and social comparisons.

Project-based learning, or problem-based learning (PBL), is a specific task-based approach that teachers can utilize to support the development of SRL. PBL focuses on student-designed inquiries of authentic problems in realistic environments that use many resources and extend over time. Marx, Blumenfeld, Karjcik, and Soloway (1997) identified five key features for implementing PBL: (a) Instructional units, which are called "projects," must be orchestrated around a driving question that is worthwhile, meaningful, and feasible; (b) projects must be in the form of investigations in which students plan, design, and conduct real-world research that includes asking questions, designing experiments, collecting and analyzing ideas, and drawing inferences; (c) students need to create artifacts that are tangible results of the investigation process and reflect their understanding; (d) projects must include collaboration with their peers as well as teachers and local experts outside of the school environment; and (e) teachers should incorporate the use of technological tools, which allow authentic investigations and support deep understandings.

If PBL activities are designed carefully with teachers who provide appropriate modeling and scaffolding, they promote and necessitate SRL. PBL affords opportunities for self-directed learning by giving students choice and control about what to work on, how to work, and what products to generate. For example, students can select their own project questions, activities, and artifacts; determine how to approach the problem and what resources to use; and how to allocate responsibility among the group (Blumenfeld et al., 1991; Marx et al., 1997). In addition to choice and control, students need to use a variety of strategies to generate and coordinate plans, to formulate and test predictions systematically, to determine solutions, and to monitor progress toward goals. Blumenfeld et al. (1991) explained that "there are at least two types of metacognition that are employed in project-based learning" (p. 379). First, moment-to-moment control and regulation of cognition is required to monitor and fine-tune thoughts while working through the details of particular tasks. Second, students need to be able to engage in strategic, purposeful thought over what may seem to be very disconnected aspects of projects to guide and control their activities. PBL promotes SRL because it places the responsibility on the students to find information, to coordinate actions and people, to reach goals, and to monitor understanding.

Students are cognitively engaged in classrooms that have open-ended tasks, projects, and problems that are based on driving questions. These are student-centered and inquiry-driven contexts in contrast to materials-driven or curriculum-driven classrooms. Tasks, teachers, and classrooms that promote intrinsic motivation, autonomy, and self-determination are likely to promote SRL among students (Deci, Vallerand, Pelletier, & Ryan, 1991). These settings foster a sense of engagement that is sometimes referred to as "flow" (Csikszentmihalyi, 1990). Flow is a satisfied state of consciousness associated with intense concentration, effortless control, and deep enjoyment. For students to be in a state of flow, challenges and skills must be aligned and sufficiently high, immediate and unambiguous feedback must be provided, and the activity must be goal-directed and allow for a sense of control (Csikszentmihalyi & Rathunde, 1993). Flow illustrates how contexts impact learners' motivational states, where motivation and SRL emerge from situations when the conditions are optimal. This kind of deep engagement elicits SRL and may require little explicit instruction or support because the nature of the activity sustains the learner's interest and effort.

SELF-ASSESSMENT

Learning depends on assessment of both product and process to know what is known, what requires additional effort, and what skills are effective. Whether elicited by others or self, assessment fosters planning and regulation of future SRL efforts (Zimmerman, 2000). Assessment of learning can have profound motivational consequences on students' classroom behavior and attitudes. Tests, exams, and grades may lead to negative outcomes for some students, especially if they have a history of poor performance, the evaluations are made public, or the students work only for extrinsic rewards. The desired positive outcomes of assessment on students include greater responsibility, sustained effort, awareness about learning, and personalized mastery goals. These are characteristic of SRL and illustrate how students' views (and theories) of assessment influence their learning. Perhaps the clearest links between SRL and assessment are seen in nonacademic arenas, such as music recitals or sports contests, where children are committed to self-improvement when faced with demonstrations of their abilities. How can academic assessments of learning be infused with the same passion and autonomy? Self-assessment may be the key.

Self-assessment includes all three domains of SRL: cognitive, motivational, and affective. Many kinds of self-assessments are possible in the classroom. Students can evaluate their levels of understanding, their personal interests, and their effort and strategies used on a task. They can assess the perceptions and attributions made by others regarding one's abilities, the improvement from one occasion to the next, the amount of assistance needed to accomplish a task, and their goals and expectations in various situations. As students learn to monitor and interpret their actions, they are able to assess a greater variety of dimensions of their behavior with more insight about possible causes and more accuracy about their progress (Paris & Cunningham, 1996; Rosenholtz & Simpson, 1984). Self-assessment involves the internalization of standards so students can regulate their own learning more effectively. When students are able to interpret their own accomplishments with pride, their perceptions of ability and efficacy increase (Zimmerman, 2000). For example, Schunk and Ertmer (2000) surmised from studies of various goals and feedback conditions that "... providing students with a learning goal and progress feedback led to the highest self-efficacy, motivated strategy use, and achievement" (p. 641). They suggest that periodic, but not too frequent, self-evaluation complements learning goals and helps students to maintain high levels of self-efficacy.

Self-assessment of learning depends on both internal and external factors. Internal factors such as metacognition enable students to reflect on their own accomplishments, to monitor their progress while learning, and to evaluate their understanding against other standards of performance. Paris and Winograd (1990) described two aspects of metacognition as self-appraisal and self-management. The former refers to review and evaluation of one's abilities, knowledge states, and cognitive strategies, whereas the latter refers to the monitoring and regulation of ongoing behavior through planning, correcting mistakes, and using fix-up strategies. Considerable research has shown that both self-appraisal and self-management of learning improve with age, intelligence, instruction, and academic achievement (e.g., Paris & Cunningham, 1996; Swanson, 1990).

External factors include the kinds of curricula and assessment activities presented to students. Instructional activities that allow little initiative, control, and independence do not allow much SRL. Such closed tasks, as opposed to open-ended tasks, foster routine responses instead of thoughtful engagement. Similarly, assessments that allow little personal responsiveness provide few opportunities for students to practice monitoring, planning, and regulating their own learning. The term *authentic assessment* is intended partly to convey the sense of assessment activities that are thought-provoking and engaging. One of the main purposes of authentic assessment is to encourage students to become involved more actively in monitoring and reviewing their own performance (Calfee, 1991; Paris & Ayres, 1994; Wiggins, 1989). This includes self-assessment of the products as well as the processes of daily learning so that students learn to reflect on their work and evaluate their effort, feelings, and accomplishments, not just their grades. Because self-assessment includes both reflection and evaluation of one's work, it helps to develop feelings of ownership and responsibility for learning. These features of students' learning are crucial in assisting students to become independent learners who develop control over their own learning.

Portfolios provide many opportunities for self-assessment through activities such as reviewing work samples, projects, and artifacts; understanding progress through record keeping; documenting interests and habits; identifying choices and preferences; conducting conferences with teachers; evaluating the processes of collaborative writing; and sharing personal responses to school work (Paris & Ayres, 1994; Tierney, Carter, & Desai, 1991). Each activity requires students to take initiative for assessing their work. Some of these activities can be done independently, whereas others are conducted with peers or teachers. There is, however, a surprising paucity of empirical research on how such activities are related to self-assessment. Van Kraayenoord and Paris (1997) investigated whether self-assessment could be measured in a brief interview. Their Work Samples Interview focused on five basic aspects of students' self-assessment. Students were asked the following: (a) to explain what work was difficult to do and what work made them proud, (b) to identify samples of their work that exhibited their literacy abilities, (c) to show evidence of their academic progress in literacy and other subjects to determine the standards that students use for self-assessment, (d) to report their feelings about self-review and their future academic development, and (e) to explain how they shared their work with parents and how they viewed feedback from teachers. These questions focus on the development of students' thinking about their learning (e.g., their knowledge, abilities, and strategies), their motivation (e.g., attributions for success, self-perceptions, and affect), their future expectations (e.g., goals, beliefs about their progress and potential improvement), and their perceptions of classroom instruction and assessment (e.g., meaningfulness, engagement, and collaboration).

The results indicated that students are able to assess their own work and provide both cognitive and affective evaluations according to particular features that influence learning (van Kraayenoord & Paris, 1997). The findings indicated that there was developmental improvement in self-assessment among 8- to 12-year-olds; older students were more able to assess their work and progress. The total scores on the Work Samples Interview were also correlated with scores on a task assessing strategic reading. Students who were able to discuss their work samples with awareness of the psychological characteristics that affect performance were more likely to be able to identify reading strategies that would enhance their comprehension and learning. Thus, the ability to assess one's work is linked to the ability to evaluate literacy strategies. This suggests that metacognitive abilities are necessary for both of these tasks. Furthermore, there were modest correlations between the Work Samples Interview and two other tasks that measured attitudes toward school and literacy habits outside school. This suggests that self-evaluation of schoolwork is linked to affective characteristics such as attitudes, interests, feelings of success at school, and enjoyment of reading and writing at home. These are positive motivational characteristics of achievement-striving students and suggest that students who are more effective at self-appraisal have more positive attitudes about school and enjoy reading and writing.

TWO METAPHORS OF SRL

There are at least two contrasting metaphors of SRL that researchers and teachers can use. One is the metaphor of acquisition, of learning new strategies and skills and then applying them in school. This is the classic view of academic strategies as specialized tools that need to be taught, practiced, and applied in school. In this view, teachers know good strategies and students do not, therefore teachers must describe them and exhort students to use them. A problem with this transmission model is that "having" a strategy does not mean that students will value or use it. Students who comply with teachers and use instructed strategies are regulated by others, not self. The transmission model of SRL raises questions in educational psychology such as, "How do teachers motivate students to use effective learning strategies? Why don't students transfer good techniques to new areas of study? Why is some knowledge inert and not enacted?" Each of these questions presupposes that teachers must change the thinking and motivation of students to make them autonomous learners. This approach is based on a model of teacher authority and directed instruction rather than a student-centered model of learning through experience and practice.

Transmission models may appear too behavioristic or simplified. There are more subtle variations of this learning model such as the "good strategy user" model (Borkowski et al., 1990) and the social learning model described by Zimmerman (2000). The latter, for example, outlines developmental levels of regulatory skill beginning with a student's observation and vicarious induction of a skill from a model and progressing through levels of emulation, self-control, and finally self-regulation. Social modeling experiences are the heart of this approach and translate into direct instructional models of SRL, or more accurately RL, because the self may not be involved in "compliant cognition." As Zimmerman (2000) noted, "Although social models are advantageous in conveying high quality methods of task skill, they may inhibit learners from assuming self-direction unless these models are phased out as soon as possible" (p. 33).

The second metaphor emphasizes "becoming" more regulated as students develop new competencies. In this view, self-regulation is a description of coherent behaviors exhibited by a person in a situation rather than a set of skills to be taught. The developmental metaphor recognizes the Piagetian tenet that behavior is organized and that self-regulation is an adaptive expression of that organization. Self-regulation in this view is not "acquired" as much as it is shaped and elaborated through participation in "zones of proximal development" according to tenets of sociocultural theories. As children develop, they are better able to coordinate actions with goals, better able to reflect on their own thinking, and better able to plan and monitor complex and abstract sequences (Deci & Ryan, 1985). These features of SRL are linked to maturation as well as the child's increasing agency in shaping psychological activities. What behaviors and thoughts become regulated to which goals, however, depend on specific experiences. These are the features of SRL linked to personal histories and situations (Ferrari & Mahalingam, 1998). In this view, SRL may be regarded not as the goal of students' learning but as the outcome of their pursuits to adapt to their unique environmental demands in a coherent manner.

We have speculated that students' coherent behavior is motivated by their desires to be recognized according to specific identities (Paris, Byrnes, & Paris, 2001). For example, some children want to please their teachers and behave as "good students" so they comply with rules and expend effort to follow teachers' directions. These students are likely to use the strategies that teachers model, discuss, and encourage because they strive for identities as successful students. Thus, the use of SRL is a consequence of the desire to be recognized as a particular identity, a "good student." This view contrasts with a view that purports that students choose goals of self-regulation, mastery, or effort. We believe that those goals are more likely to be superficial and deliberate than underlying identity strivings in which self-regulation is both a means and an outcome to more fundamental goals but not a goal in itself. Desires to display competence, to gain acceptance, or to be perceived as a particular "possible self" (Markus & Nurius, 1986) are the primary motivational influences. Those strivings may be enacted in various ways.

Desire is not enough, however, because identity strivings must be accompanied by feelings that the identity is possible and valuable to achieve (Bandura, 1997; Higgins, 1991). Students may exhibit regulated actions as they try out various possible selves and the roles associated with them. What motivates action is the desire to be recognized as the smart student, the fast work-finisher, or the quiet–serious intellectual. These possible selves all lead to SRL typically associated with good strategy users and good students. However, students might also strive for identities rejected by teachers such as the practical joker, the bully, or the cheat. Students can be highly regulated in pursuit of these identities as well. Regardless of the particular role that the person is trying to enact, the self-regulated actions are intended to confirm this specific identity for the audience of others as well as for the individual.

Striving to enact an identity, fueled by desires to be recognized and validated as a specific kind of self, provide coherence to a person's actions. The behaviors that appear planned, regulated, and monitored, are subservient to these underlying motives. Such a view incorporates both intrinsic and extrinsic motivation. Identity strivings can be strengthened by extrinsic rewards, such as getting a high grade on a test, as well as vicarious reinforcement, such as seeing a peer rewarded for the aspired achievements or behavior. However, striving for discrete subgoals and rewards may not be obvious to students who simply want to be viewed in a particular way by valued others. Intrinsic motivation, such as sustained interest and "flow" experiences, may contribute to long-term strivings because of the satisfaction of engaging in activities of the desired self. Participation in practices of the desired self demonstrates both competence and membership, strengthening both the I–self as agent and the Me–self as identity, which provides positive feedback to continue as well as motivation to display the practices. The outward appearance is actions that are highly self-directed and regulated.

Both metaphors of SRL may be useful because they focus on processes of learning, development, and instruction. The transmission view requires teachers to provide explicit information about effective SRL practices and to structure the environment to allow opportunities to practice and generalize the strategies. The developmental view requires teachers to analyze how students regulate their own behavior and to understand students' aspired identities as precursors to shaping their SRL toward academic goals. The latter view suggests that SRL becomes more meaningful to students when academic goals and strategies are tied to their deeper strivings to display competence as achieving students. Regardless of the perspective one takes, students become more self-regulated with age, experience, opportunity, and desire. For those students who adopt academic goals, SRL involves positive academic strategies and results in success in school. Teachers need to provide direct explanations about SRL, multiple curriculum opportunities that foster SRL, and positive models of self-regulated learners so that students can aspire to learn and use effective strategies for their own education.

PRINCIPLES OF SRL TO APPLY IN CLASSROOMS

Paris and Winograd (1999) described 12 principles that teachers can use to design activities in classrooms that promote students' SRL. They provide a useful summary of the research we discussed and may make the applications of SRL to classrooms more direct, therefore a list follows. We organized them according to four major features of research on SRL with corollaries following each one:

1. Self-appraisal leads to a deeper understanding of learning.
   a. Analyzing personal styles and strategies of learning, and comparing them with the strategies of others, increases personal awareness of different ways of learning.
   b. Evaluating what you know and what you do not know, as well as discerning your personal depth of understanding about key points, promotes efficient effort allocation.
   c. Periodic self-assessment of learning processes and outcomes is a useful habit to develop because it promotes monitoring of progress, stimulates repair strategies, and promotes feelings of self-efficacy.
2. Self-management of thinking, effort, and affect promotes flexible approaches to problem solving that are adaptive, persistent, self-controlled, strategic, and goal-oriented.
   a. Setting appropriate goals that are attainable yet challenging are most effective when chosen by the individual and when they embody a mastery orientation rather than a performance goal.
   b. Managing time and resources through effective planning and monitoring is essential to setting priorities, overcoming frustration, and persisting to task completion.
   c. Reviewing one's own learning, revising the approach, or even starting anew, may indicate self-monitoring and a personal commitment to high standards of performance.
3. Self-regulation can be taught in diverse ways.
   a. Self-regulation can be taught with explicit instruction, directed reflection, metacognitive discussions, and participation in practices with experts.
   b. Self-regulation can be promoted indirectly by modeling and by activities that entail reflective analyses of learning.

c. Self-regulation can be promoted by assessing, charting, and discussing evidence of personal growth.

4. Self-regulation is woven into the narrative experiences and the identity strivings of each individual.
   a. How individuals choose to appraise and monitor their own behavior is usually consistent with their preferred or desired identity.
   b. Gaining an autobiographical perspective on education and learning provides a narrative framework that deepens personal awareness of self-regulation.
   c. Participation in a reflective community enhances the frequency and depth of examination of one's self-regulation habits.

ENDURING ISSUES ABOUT SRL AND FUTURE DIRECTIONS FOR RESEARCH

We think SRL is a synthesis of many constructs in learning and motivation and has direct relevance for teachers. We highlighted literacy instruction, cognitive engagement, and self-assessment as three areas in which SRL research has direct applications in classrooms. However, teachers can extend the same principles of SRL to educational technology, to study skills, to scientific reasoning, and many other academic arenas. Our enthusiasm for SRL is based on the functional and pragmatic aspects of this line of inquiry for students of all ages. It is tempered by concerns for abiding issues that invite future research. We identify three broad issues with the following questions.

What Does it Mean for Students to be Self-Regulated?

Most important, self-regulated students display motivated actions, that is, goal-directed and controlled behaviors that they apply to specific situations. SRL is the fusion of skill and will (McCombs & Marzano, 1990; Paris & Cross, 1983). It is informed by metacognition from self and others and is fueled by affect and desire. However, we need more research on the "hot cognitions and motivation" that energize students. Are they motivated to display their competence, to impress others, to acquire good grades, to win respect of teachers and parents, or to avoid shame and embarrassment? Of course, all these factors might motivate students, but we need to examine how individuals become motivated to be self-regulated. Research should focus on the developmental characteristics of SRL as well as the individual differences.

How students exhibit SRL is as much of an issue as why they display it. Historically, SRL has been regarded as a set of positive learning strategies that good students apply judiciously. However, such a characterization emphasizes the acquisition of instrumental tactics and the approach of positive goals such as studying text, revising one's writing, or monitoring one's problem solving. Some students can be instrumental in using tactics that lead to less noble outcomes. For example, if a student has failed high-stakes multiple-choice tests for several years, he or she might feel pessimistic, helpless, or angry when given another such test. To avoid another threat to self-esteem or potential confirmation of low ability, the student might pretend to become ill, give a half-hearted effort, or cheat. These actions might be deliberate and goal-oriented, although not in a positive manner, and thus would also be SRL. SRL can involve avoidance of behaviors as well as approach. For example, a student might be highly regulated to avoid distractions while studying or avoid peers who pull them off task. A less aspiring student could be self-regulated in avoiding hard work or studying altogether and spend his time fabricating an excuse. Self-handicapping techniques are clearly the outcome of motivated actions designed to minimize threats to self-esteem (Covington, 1992). Thus, self-regulated actions may be directed to the attainment or avoidance of goals that are held in either high or low regard by teachers.

How Do Students Become Self-Regulated?

We believe that every student constructs his or her own theory of SRL. This theory can be naïve and ill-informed or elaborate and appropriate. Indeed, children's theories of SRL, that is, what they must do to achieve specific goals in specific contexts, probably change like their theories of mind, school, and self (Harter, 1999; Paris & Cunningham, 1996). We think that children's understanding of SRL is enhanced in three ways: indirectly through experience, directly through instruction, and elicited through practice. First, SRL can be induced from authentic or repeated experiences in school. For example, students may realize that checking their work does not require much additional time and leads to greater accuracy. For many students, SRL may emerge as tacit knowledge about what is expected by the teacher and what is useful behavior for the student. Second, teachers may provide explicit instruction about SRL. SRL is directly taught, for example, when a teacher describes the need to analyze each term in a story problem in math, place them in the proper location, perform the arithmetic calculation on them, and check the answer (Greeno & Goldman, 1998; Schoenfeld, 1992). SRL instruction could emphasize detailed strategy instruction or it might involve increasing students' awareness about appropriate motivational goals and standards. Explicit instruction designed to avoid distractions and persevere in the face of difficulty is an example of volitional control that promotes SRL (Corno, 1993).

Third, we believe that SRL can be acquired through engagement in practices that require self-regulation, that is, in situations in which self-regulation is welded to the nature of the task. For example, collaborative learning projects often require each student to contribute one part of the overall project. If a student's contribution is inadequate, the need for further work and the direction of the improvement may become apparent in the process of working on the project. It could also be pointed out explicitly by peers but the self-regulation aspect may be required as part of the activity. This is the intent of creating "communities of learners" that is consistent with learning through participation and practice (Brown & Campione, 1990; Lave, 1991; Rogoff et al., 1995). Rarely would we expect SRL to be acquired neatly in only one of these three manners: indirect induction, direct instruction, and elicited actions. All three probably operate together in classrooms as children create their theories about learning in school and their own abilities as they work with teachers, parents, and peers.

Are There Individual Differences in SRL?

More attention needs to be given to the differences among children in SRL. Research shows that children in primary grades exhibit less SRL than children in later grades, however, this is a consequence of many factors, including age, cognitive development, explicit instruction, and changing demands in the classroom. It is possible that personality differences in impulsivity, activity levels, patience, resistance to distractions, and internal locus of control might contribute to differences in SRL. Students who have difficulty using strategies and maintaining task focus and engagement may need more explicit instruction and support to promote SRL (Englert, Raphael, Anderson, Anthony, & Stevens, 1991; Graham, 1997). It is not clear why some students are more comfortable than others when it comes to monitoring their behavior, double-checking their answers, talking about their own thinking, or writing reflective journals. Some students simply may have greater capacities than others for monitoring and regulating their behaviors.

There are also intraindividual factors that need additional research. For example, capacity for SRL may vary between students but it almost certainly varies within students during the school day and year. Some students may be more vigilant in the morning than afternoon; some may be more careful in reading than math; and some may be more careful when they are interested in the subject matter. SRL requires effort to be vigilant and strategic and it is reasonable to assume that students cannot be vigilant and focused without periodic rests. Cognitive fatigue must contribute to the lack of SRL just as alertness probably fosters better attention. Teachers understand this and research may help identify how periods of vigilance can be spaced among tasks and time to promote SRL.

Perhaps the greatest source of individual difference lies in the failures to self-regulate thinking and behavior. Lack of knowledge and experience are the usual explanations for students' poor self-regulation. However, when children do not induce effective monitoring and regulation from academic tasks and direct instruction, teachers might infer that the students have a learning or attention disorder. Indeed, there may be neurological and personality factors that underlie failures in self-control (Baumeister, Heatherton, & Tice, 1994). Mood, affect, impulsivity, impatience, and aggression may also prevent some students from appraising and managing their own behavior. Such factors may be considerably more resistant to change than lack of appropriate goal orientations or knowledge about useful strategies.

CONCLUSION

We showed how research in educational psychology has studied and promoted SRL in classrooms. Direct explanations about cognitive strategies, metacognitive discussions, and peer tutoring can all help increase students' use of effective learning strategies. SRL is also more likely when teachers create classroom environments in which students have opportunities to seek challenges, to reflect on their progress, and to take responsibility and pride in their accomplishments. SRL then is a combination of knowledge about appropriate actions coupled with motivation to pursue goals supported in environments that allow students to be autonomous. Clearly, SRL is more than a developmental milestone tied to grade levels or an educational achievement tied to specific learning. Both experience and context contribute to SRL.

Teachers can use knowledge about SRL directly in several ways. First, students of all ages can benefit from analyses and discussions of strategies for learning. Young children might discuss how to use pictures as clues to text meaning, whereas college students might discuss alternative ways to take notes, but they are both metacognitive discussions about regulating learning. Teachers need to be able to describe appropriate strategies—what they are, how they operate, and when they should be applied—and be able to lead discussions so that students can explore their understanding about how they learn. Second, teachers can design open-ended instructional activities and scaffold assistance for student inquiry. Less emphasis should be placed on workbook exercises and routine tasks and more emphases should be placed on working together to guide students to more effective approaches to learning. Third, teachers can minimize objective tests (e.g., multiple-choice tests, true–false tests), competitive test scores, and public comparisons of performance which detract from students' sense of efficacy and mastery. Projects, portfolios, and performance assessments can motivate students, provide opportunities for SRL, and enhance creative expression. Linking self-assessment with external standards may help students regulate their actions to desired outcomes. These practical suggestions for helping children take charge of their own learning are direct manifestations of research on SRL. The synergy between practices in classrooms and research on SRL should be useful for many years.

REFERENCES

Alexander, P. (1995). Superimposing a situation-specific and domain-specific perspective on an account of self-regulated learning. *Educational Psychologist, 30,* 189–193.

Bandura, A. (1997). *Self-efficacy: The exercise of control.* New York: Freeman.

Baumann, J. F. (1984). The effectiveness of a direct instruction paradigm for teaching main idea comprehension. *Reading Research Quarterly, 20,* 93–115.

Baumeister, R. F., Heatherton, T. F., & Tice, D. M. (1994). *Losing control: How and why people fail at self-regulation.* San Diego, CA: Academic.

Blumenfeld, P. (1992). Classroom learning and motivation: Clarifying and expanding goal theory. *Journal of Educational Psychology, 84,* 272–281.

Blumenfeld, P., Hamilton, V., Bossert, S., Wessels, K., & Meece, J. (1983). Teacher talk and student thought: Socialization into the student role. In J. M. Levine & M. C. Wang (Eds.), *Teacher and student perceptions: Implications for learning* (pp. 143–192). Hillsdale, NJ: Lawrence Erlbaum Associates, Inc.

Blumenfeld, P. C., Mergendoller, J. R., & Swarthout, D. W. (1987). Task as a heuristic for understanding student learning and motivation. *Journal of Curriculum Studies, 19,* 135–148.

Blumenfeld, P. C., Soloway, E., Marx, R. W., Krajcik, J. S., Guzdial, M., & Palincsar, A. S. (1991). Motivating project-based learning: Sustaining the doing, supporting the learning. *Educational Psychologist, 26,* 369–398.

Boekaerts, M. (1998). Do culturally rooted self-construals affect students' conceptualization of control over learning? *Educational Psychologist, 33,* 87–108.

Borkowski, J., Carr, M., Rellinger, E., & Pressley, M. (1990). Self-regulated cognition: Interdependence of metacognition, attributions, and self-esteem. In B.F. Jones & L. Idol (Eds.), *Dimensions of thinking and cognitive instruction* (pp. 53–92). Hillsdale, NJ: Lawrence Erlbaum Associates, Inc.

Brophy, J. (Ed.). (1999). The value aspects of motivation in education [Special issue]. *Educational Psychologist, 34.*

Brown, A. L. (1978). Knowing when, where, and how to remember. A problem of metacognition. In R. Glaser (Ed.), Advances in instructional psychology (Vol. 1, pp. 77–165). Hillsdale, NJ: Lawrence Erlbaum Associates, Inc.

Brown, A. L., & Campione, J. C. (1990). Communities of learning and thinking, or a context by any other name. *Human Development, 21,* 108–125.

Brown, A., & Day, J. (1983). Macrorules for summarizing text: The development of expertise. *Journal of Verbal Learning and Verbal Behavior, 22,* 1–14.

Calfee, R. C. (1991). Authentic assessment of elementary literacy: A question of realities. *Kamehameha Journal of Education, 2,* 71–76.

Connell, J., & Wellborn, J. (1991). Competence, autonomy, and relatedness: A motivational analysis of self-system processes. In M. Gunnar & L. A. Sroufe (Eds.), *Self processes and development* (Vol. 23, pp. 43–77). Hillsdale, NJ: Lawrence Erlbaum Associates, Inc.

Corno, L. (1993). The best-laid plans. *Educational Researcher, 22*(2), 14–22.

Covington, M. V. (1992). *Making the grade: A self-worth perspective on motivation and school reform.* Cambridge, England: Cambridge University Press.

Csikszentmihalyi, M. (1990). *Flow: The psychology of optimal experience.* New York: HarperCollins.

Csikszentmihalyi, M., & Rathunde, K. (1993). The measurement of flow in everyday life: Toward a theory of emergent motivation. In J. E. Jacobs (Ed.), *Developmental perspectives on motivation: Nebraska symposium on motivation* (pp. 57–97). Lincoln: University of Nebraska Press.

Deci, E. L., & Ryan, R. M. (1985). *Intrinsic motivation and self-determination in human behavior.* New York: Plenum.

Deci, E. L., Vallerand, R. J., Pelletier, L. G., & Ryan, R. M. (1991). Motivation and education: The self-determination perspective. *Educational Psychologist, 26,* 325–346.

Doyle, W. (1983). Academic work. *Review of Educational Research, 53,* 159–200.

Englert, C. S., Raphael, T. E., Anderson, L. M., Anthony, H. M., & Stevens, D. D. (1991). Making strategies and self-talk visible: Writing instruction in regular and special education classrooms. *American Educational Research Journal, 28,* 337–372.

Ferrari, M., & Mahalingam, R. (1998). Personal cognitive development and its implications for teaching and learning. *Educational Psychologist, 33,* 35–44.

Graham, S. (1997). Executive control in the revising of students with learning and writing difficulties. *Journal of Educational Psychology, 89,* 223–234.

Greeno, J., & Goldman, S. (Eds.). (1998). *Thinking practices in mathematics and science learning.* Mahwah, NJ: Lawrence Erlbaum Associates, Inc.

Grolnick, W. S., Kurowski, C. O., & Gurland, S. T. (1999). Family processes and the development of children's self-regulation. *Educational Psychologist, 34,* 3–14.

Harris, K. R., & Graham, S. (1992). *Helping young writers master the craft: Strategy instruction and self-regulation in the writing process.* Cambridge, MA: Brookline Books.

Harris, K. R., & Graham, S. (1996). *Making the writing process work: Strategies for composition and self-regulation.* Cambridge, MA: Brookline Books.

Harter, S. (1999). *The construction of self.* New York: Guilford.

Higgins, E. T. (1991). Development of self-regulatory and self-evaluative processes: Costs, benefits, and tradeoffs. In M. R. Gunnar & L. A. Sroufe (Eds.), *Self processes and development: The Minnesota symposia on child development* (Vol. 23, pp. 125–166). Hillsdale, NJ: Lawrence Erlbaum Associates, Inc.

Johnston, P., & Afflerbach, P. (1985). The process of constructing main ideas from text. *Cognition & Instruction, 2,* 207–232.

Kuhl, J. (1984). Volitional aspects of achievement motivation and learned helplessness: Toward a comprehensive theory of action control. In B. A. Maher (Ed.), *Progress in experimental personality research* (Vol. 12, pp. 99–170). New York: Academic.

Lave, J. (1991). Situating learning in communities of practice. In L. B. Resnick, J. M. Levine, & S. D. Teasley (Eds.), *Perspectives on socially shared cognition* (pp. 63–82). Washington, DC: American Psychological Association.

Levin, J. R., & Pressley, M. (Eds.). (1986). Learning strategies [Special issue]. *Educational Psychologist, 21,* 3–17.

Marks, H., Doane, K., & Secada, W. (1996). Support for student achievement. In F. M. Newmann (Ed.), *Authentic achievement: Restructuring schools for intellectual quality* (pp. 209–227). San Francisco: Jossey-Bass.

Markus, H., & Nurius, P. (1986). Possible selves. *American Psychologist, 41,* 954–969.

Marx, R., Blumenfeld, P., Krajcik, J., & Soloway, E. (1997). Enacting project-based science. *Elementary School Journal, 97,* 341–358.

McCombs, B. L., & Marzano, R. J. (1990). Putting the self in self-regulated learning: The self as agent in integrating will and skill. *Educational Psychologist, 25,* 51–69.

Newmann, F., Wehlage, G., & Lamborn, S. (1992). The significance and sources of student engagement. In F. Newmann (Ed.), *Student engagement and achievement in American secondary schools* (pp. 11–39). New York: Teachers College Press.

Page-Voth, V., & Graham, S. (1999). Effects of goal setting and strategy use on the writing performance and self-efficacy of students with writing and learning problems. *Journal of Educational Psychology, 91,* 230–240.

Palincsar, A. S., & Brown, A. (1984). Reciprocal teaching of comprehension-fostering and comprehension-monitoring activities. *Cognition and Instruction, 1,* 117–175.

Paris, S. G. (Ed.). (1987). Current issues in reading comprehension [Special issue]. *Educational Psychologist, 22.*

Paris, S. G., & Ayres, L. R. (1994). *Becoming reflective students and teachers with portfolios and authentic assessment.* Washington, DC: American Psychological Association.

Paris, S. G., Byrnes, J. P., & Paris, A. H. (2001). Constructing theories, identities, and actions of self-regulated learners. In B. Zimmerman & D. Schunk (Eds.), *Self-regulated learning and academic achievement* (pp. 253–287). New York: Springer-Verlag.

Paris, S. G., & Cross, D. R. (1983). Ordinary learning: Pragmatic connections among children's beliefs, motives, and actions. In J. Bisanz, G. Bisanz, & R. Kail (Eds.), *Learning in children* (pp. 137–169). New York: Springer-Verlag.

Paris, S. G., Cross, D. R., & Lipson, M. Y. (1984). Informed strategies for learning: A program to improve children's reading awareness and comprehension. *Journal of Educational Psychology, 76*, 1239–1252.

Paris, S. G., & Cunningham, A. (1996). Children becoming students. In D. Berliner & R. Calfee (Eds.), *Handbook of educational psychology* (pp. 117–147). New York: Macmillan.

Paris, S. G., Lipson, M. Y., & Wixson, K. (1983). Becoming a strategic reader. *Contemporary Educational Psychology, 8*, 293–316.

Paris, S., & Newman, R. (1990). Developmental aspects of self-regulated learning. *Educational Psychologist, 25*, 87–102.

Paris, S. G., & Turner, J. C. (1994). Situated motivation. In P. Pintrich, D. Brown, & C. Weinstein (Eds.), *Student motivation, cognition, and learning: Essays in honor of Wilbert J. McKeachie* (pp. 213–237). Hillsdale, NJ: Lawrence Erlbaum Associates, Inc.

Paris, S. G., Wasik, B. A., & Turner, J. C. (1991). The development of strategic readers. In R. Barr, M. Kamil, P. Mosenthal, & P. D. Pearson (Eds.), *Handbook of reading research* (2nd ed., pp. 609–640). New York: Longman.

Paris, S. G., & Winograd, P. (1990). How metacognition can promote academic learning and instruction. In B. J. Jones & L. Idol (Eds.), *Dimensions of thinking and cognitive instruction* (pp. 15–51). Hillsdale, NJ: Lawrence Erlbaum Associates, Inc.

Paris, S. G., & Winograd, P. (1999). *The role of self-regulated learning in contextual teaching: Principles and practices for teacher preparation. Contextual teaching and learning: Preparing teachers to enhance student success in the workplace and beyond* (Information Series No. 376). Columbus, OH: ERIC Clearinghouse on Adult, Career, and Vocational Education; Washington, DC: ERIC Clearinghouse on Teaching and Teacher Education.

Paris, S. G., Wixson, K. K., & Palincsar, A. M. (1986). Instructional approaches to reading comprehension. In E. Rothkopf (Ed.), *Review of research in education* (pp. 91–128). Washington, DC: American Educational Research Association.

Patrick, H. (1997). Social self-regulation: Exploring the relations between children's social relationships, academic self-regulation, and school performance. *Educational Psychologist, 32*, 209–220.

Pintrich, P. R. (2000). The role of goal orientation in self-regulated learning. In M. Boekaerts, P. Pintrich, & M. Zeidner (Eds.), *Handbook of self-regulation* (pp. 452–502). New York: Academic.

Pintrich, P. R., & DeGroot, E. V. (1990). Motivational and self-regulated learning components of classroom academic performance. *Journal of Educational Psychology, 82*, 33–40.

Pressley, M. (1995). More about the development of self-regulation: Complex, long-term, and thoroughly social. *Educational Psychologist, 30*, 207–212.

Pressley, M. Almasi, J., Schuder, T., Bergman, J., & Kurita, J. A. (1994). Transactional instruction of comprehension strategies: The Montgomery County Maryland SAIL program. *Reading and Writing Quarterly: Overcoming Learning Difficulties, 10*, 5–19.

Pressley, M., & Ghatala, E. S. (1990). Self-regulated learning: Monitoring learning from text. *Educational Psychologist, 25*, 19–33.

Pressley, M., Harris, K. R., & Marks, M. B. (1992). But good strategy instructors are constructivists! *Educational Psychology Review, 4*, 3–31.

Pressley, M., Johnson, C. J., Symons, S., McGoldrick, J. A., & Kurita, J. A. (1989). Strategies that improve children's memory and comprehension of text. *Elementary School Journal, 90*, 3–32.

Rogoff, B., Baker-Sennett, J., Lacasa, P., & Goldsmith, D. (1995). Development through participation in sociocultural activity. In J. J. Goodnow, P. J. Miller, & F. Kessel (Eds.), *Cultural practices as contexts for development* (pp. 45–65). San Francisco: Jossey-Bass.

Rosenholtz, S. J., & Simpson, C. (1984). The formation of ability conceptions: Developmental trend or social construction? *Review of Educational Research, 54*, 31–63.

Schoenfeld, A. (1992). Learning to think mathematically: Problem solving, metacognition and sense making in mathematics. In D. Grouws (Ed.), *Handbook of research on mathematics teaching and learning: A project of the National Council of Teaching of Mathematics* (pp. 334–370). New York: Macmillan.

Schunk, D. H., & Ertmer, P.A. (2000). Self-regulation and academic learning: Self-efficacy enhancing interventions. In M. Boekaerts, P. Pintrich, & M. Zeidner (Eds.), *Handbook of self-regulation* (pp. 631–649). New York: Academic.

Stipek, D., Feiler, R., Daniels, D., & Milburn, S. (1995). Effects of different instructional approaches on young children's achievement and motivation. *Child Development, 66*, 209–223.

Swanson, H. L. (1990). Influence of metacognitive knowledge and aptitude on problem-solving. *Journal of Educational Psychology, 82*, 306–314.

Tierney, R. L., Carter, M. A., & Desai, L. E. (1991). *Portfolios in the reading-writing classroom.* Norwood, MA: Christopher Gordon.

Turner, J. C. (1995). The influence of classroom contexts on young children's motivation for literacy. *Reading Research Quarterly, 30*, 410–441.

van Kraayenoord, C. E., & Paris, S. G. (1997). Children's self-appraisal of their worksamples and academic progress. *Elementary School Journal, 97*, 523–537.

Weinstein, C., & Mayer, R. (1986). The teaching of learning strategies. In M. Wittrock (Ed.), *Handbook of research on teaching* (pp. 315–327). New York: Macmillan.

Wehlage, G. (1989). Educational engagement. In G. Wehlage, R. Rutter, G. Smith, & N. Lesko (Eds.), *Reducing the risk: Schools as communities of support* (pp. 176–195). London: Falmer.

Wentzel, K. R., & Berndt, T. J. (Eds.). (1999). Social influences on school adjustment: Families, peers, neighborhoods, and culture [Special issue]. *Educational Psychologist, 34.*

Wiggins, G. (1989). A true test: Toward more authentic and equitable assessment. *Phi Delta Kappan, 70*, 703–713.

Winograd, P. N. (1984). Strategic difficulties in summarizing texts. *Reading Research Quarterly, 19*, 404–425.

Zimmerman, B. J. (Ed.). (1990). Self-regulated learning and academic achievement [Special issue]. *Educational Psychologist, 25*, 3–17.

Zimmerman, B. J. (2000). Attaining self-regulation: A social cognitive perspective. In M. Boekarts, P. Pintrich, & M. Zeidner (Eds.), *Self-regulation: Theory, research, and applications* (pp. 13–39). Orlando, FL: Academic.

Zimmerman, B. J., & Schunk, D. (1989). *Self-regulated learning and academic achievement.* New York: Springer-Verlag.

Zimmerman, B. J., & Schunk, D. (2001). *Self-regulated learning and academic achievement.* New York: Springer-Verlag.

EDUCATIONAL PSYCHOLOGIST, *36*(2), 103–112

Classroom Management: A Critical Part of Educational Psychology, With Implications for Teacher Education

Edmund T. Emmer
Department of Educational Psychology
The University of Texas at Austin

Laura M. Stough
Department of Educational Psychology
Texas A&M University

Research on classroom management is reviewed, with an emphasis on lines of inquiry originating in educational psychology with implications for teacher education. Preventive, group based approaches to management provide a basis for teachers to plan and organize classroom activities and behaviors. Studies of teacher expertise and affect provide additional perspective on teacher development and on factors that influence management. Cooperative learning activities and inclusion of children with special needs illustrate particular contexts that affect management. Utilization of classroom management content in educational psychology components of teacher preparation is discussed.

Classroom management has been an important area in educational psychology for some time. Research findings have been applied to inservice and to preservice teacher preparation programs, as well as to systems of teacher assessment and evaluation. Classroom management also represents a significant aspect of the teacher's pedagogical knowledge and is often found as a component of taxonomies and descriptions of core knowledge for educators (e.g., Council for Exceptional Children, 1998). Some researchers have suggested, moreover, that novice teachers may need to reach a minimum level of competency in management skills before they are able to develop in other areas of instruction (Berliner, 1988). Classroom management thus merits careful attention by educational psychologists who are interested in their discipline's impact on education.

WHAT IS CLASSROOM MANAGEMENT?

Definitions of classroom management vary, but usually include actions taken by the teacher to establish order, engage students, or elicit their cooperation. For example, the working definition used in a National Society for the Study of Education Yearbook on the topic (Duke, 1979) follows: "The provisions and procedures necessary to establish and maintain an environment in which instruction and learning can occur" (p. xii). More recently, the conceptualization has been expanded by delineating both the complexity of the setting in which the strategies and procedures are enacted, as well as the scope of the teacher's goals in carrying out management behaviors. For example, Doyle (1986) summarized it as "The actions and strategies teachers use to solve the problem of order in classrooms" (p. 397). Building on Jackson's (1968) analysis of classroom life, he noted that management's complexity results from several properties of classroom teaching, including multidimensionality (varied events and persons), simultaneity (many things happen at once), immediacy (the rapid pace of events limits reflection), unpredictability (of events and outcomes), publicness (events are often witnessed by many or all students), and history (actions and events have pasts and futures). Jones (1996) emphasized the comprehensive nature of classroom management by identifying five main features:

1. An understanding of current research and theory in classroom management and students' psychological and learning needs.
2. The creation of positive teacher–student and peer relationships.

Requests for reprints should be sent to Edmund T. Emmer, Department of Educational Psychology, The University of Texas at Austin, TX 78712. E-mail: emmer@mail.utexas.edu

3. The use of instructional methods that facilitate optimal learning by responding to the academic needs of individual students and the classroom group.
4. The use of organizational and group management methods that maximize on-task behavior.
5. The ability to use a range of counseling and behavioral methods to assist students who demonstrate persistent or serious behavior problems (p. 507).

This broad view of classroom management encompasses both establishing and maintaining order, designing effective instruction, dealing with students as a group, responding to the needs of individual students, and effectively handling the discipline and adjustment of individual students. Similarly to Jones (1996), most authors of texts on classroom management adopt a comprehensive view, although the inclusion of Jones' third item, choosing methods of facilitating optimal learning, makes management difficult to distinguish from teaching in general.

Most research on classroom management has attempted to identify teacher strategies and behaviors that optimize one or more of the goals of management. Although multiple and broadly defined goals would be ideal, most researchers have had to cope with the unfeasibility of assessing a wide array of outcomes in a large enough sample of classrooms to produce dependable explanations for observed results. Consequently, although some studies have used student achievement or attitudes as outcomes, most management research has been concerned with identifying how teachers bring about student engagement and limit disruption.

The rationale for adopting behavioral outcomes as criteria for defining managerial effectiveness is that they can be empirically connected to achievement outcomes (see discussion later), and also because there is a logical argument for their validity. Regardless of the nature of a given learning task, it makes sense that students must be engaged in order for learning to occur. Thus, on-task behavior is a reasonable goal of management. Furthermore, disruptive behavior is likely to interfere with instructional activities and to distract other students from learning. Good classroom management, then, is viewed as a condition for student learning, by allowing teachers to accomplish other important instructional goals. Kounin (1970), for example, noted

> The focus upon group management skills actually enables the teacher to program for individual differences and to help individual children. If there is a climate of work involvement and freedom from deviancy, different groups of children may be doing different things, and the teacher is free to help individual children. (p. 145)

Although we think this is a reasonable point of view, it does not necessarily follow that students in an orderly classroom environment will accomplish all of the other instructional goals identified with some comprehensive definitions of classroom management. In particular, as McCaslin and Good (1992, 1998) discussed, some classroom management systems might be at odds with instructional or curricular goals. For example, rule-and-consequence based systems, such Canter and Canter's (1976) initial version of Assertive Discipline, may limit student opportunities for choice and participation in classroom governance. In such classrooms, attempts to help students become self-regulated learners would be inconsistent with the direction of authority in a teacher–student relationship. The management style that teachers employ should be congruent to the teachers' instructional goals for their students, the types of activities used in the classroom, and the characteristics of the students themselves. Ideally, management and instruction are adapted by reflective teachers to take such factors into account. More classroom research, such as that of Allen (1986), would help clarify the complex interplay between management approaches and individual student goals.

Significant Lines of Inquiry

Contemporary classroom management research was substantially influenced by the studies of Jacob Kounin and his colleagues (1970). Kounin's work was conducted in the tradition of ecological psychology (cf. Jacob, 1987), which focused on determining, within specific behavior settings, environmental conditions that influenced behavior. Kounin's early studies examined desist events following inappropriate behaviors. After determining that the nature of desists was not consistently predictive of managerial effectiveness, he identified a set of teacher behaviors and lesson characteristics, including withitness, smoothness, momentum, overlapping, and group alerting, that were associated with student work involvement and freedom from deviancy. Kounin was also interested in questions that seem surprisingly contemporary, such as whether managerial behaviors that work for regular students have the same effects on students identified as emotionally disturbed in the same classrooms. His answer was "yes," at least in whole class behavior settings in regular classrooms (Kounin & Obradovic, 1968). Kounin's work helped shift the focus of management research from reactive strategies to preventive strategies and from teacher personality to the environmental and strategic components of management. His work also highlighted the influence of classroom activities as a source of important variations in student and teacher behavior. Other research in the ecological psychology tradition, including work on classroom seating arrangements (cf. Lambert, 1994) and on transition management (Arlin, 1979), contributed to this line of inquiry.

Process–outcome research during the 70s also served as impetus for examining classroom management. Studies in this tradition targeted teacher behaviors that predicted student outcomes, primarily student achievement gains. For example, Brophy, Evertson, and colleagues (Anderson, Evertson, & Brophy, 1979; Brophy & Evertson, 1976) initiated a series of large-scale process–outcome studies in elementary and junior high or middle school classrooms. Some of the more consistent correlates of student achievement gains in these studies were managerial behaviors, such as monitoring student behavior, communicating clear expectations, keeping students engaged in academic tasks, and minimizing disruptions. Similarly, other classroom-based research found relations between managerial aspects of teaching behavior and achievement outcomes. Good and Grouws (1977) conducted an extensive program of research on elementary grade mathematics instruction. They found that teachers whose classes had greater achievement gains had better management skills, and that they spent less time in transitions and dealing with discipline problems. Such teachers also managed instructional activities more effectively, by keeping activities moving at a brisk pace and by providing clear explanations and directions. Another series of studies conducted by the Soars (Soar & Soar, 1979) highlighted the importance of effective management in the classroom. These studies differentiated among management of student behavior, learning tasks, and thinking, noting that what may be optimal control varies across these domains. They noted that higher levels of control over student behaviors such as movement and talk were associated with higher achievement, but that the relation was curvilinear for student thinking and for learning tasks.

Building on the identification of the importance of classroom management in the process–outcome research literature, a series of field studies was conducted to better understand important managerial features and properties, and how they were established and maintained. Initial studies were done in 27 elementary and 51 junior high or middle school classrooms (Anderson, Evertson, & Emmer, 1980; Emmer, Evertson, & Anderson, 1980; Evertson & Emmer, 1982). Influenced by the need to describe carefully the teachers' managerial activities in their classroom context, qualitative data, including extensive observer field notes and interviews with teachers, were also collected. Another important feature of these studies was the extensive use of classroom observation at the beginning of the school year, at which time, it was hypothesized, important managerial tasks took place. Groups of more and less effective classroom mangers were identified and compared, using process measures, descriptive analyses, and teacher interview data, to describe aspects of good classroom management. In addition, classroom management in important contexts, such as lower socioeconomic status classrooms (Sanford & Evertson, 1981) and highly heterogeneous classes (Evertson, Sanford, & Emmer, 1981), was examined and described.

Although some of the details varied with grade level, subject, and socioeconomic background of students, the concepts and principles that emerged presented a coherent picture of how a well-managed setting is created. Two key principles follow: (a) good management is preventive rather than reactive, and (b) teachers help create well-managed classrooms by identifying and teaching desirable behaviors to their students. At the beginning of the school year, effective teachers had a clear conception of what student behaviors were desired, and they taught these expectations to students in several ways. They established rules or guidelines for desired behaviors; they planned and taught routines and procedures for class activities to students (a task that could take several weeks in complex settings); and they monitored student behavior and work carefully, so that initial problems were detected and corrected before inappropriate behavior could become established. The emphasis during the first few weeks of instruction was to provide successful academic experiences, with feedback to students designed to help them learn desirable behavior in the context of their academic activities. This early emphasis resulted in a more positive climate and student cooperation throughout the year. Effective teachers maintained their management system by monitoring and providing prompt feedback, pacing class activities to keep them moving, and by consistently applying classroom procedures and consequences.

The next studies were two field experiments in which groups of teachers in four school districts participated in beginning-of-year workshops and received training in the management principles and concepts identified in the previous studies. In comparison to random control groups, experimental group teachers utilized more of the recommended managerial behaviors and their classrooms had higher levels of student engagement and cooperation. These studies also extended and corroborated findings on dimensions of management derived from the prior studies (e.g., Evertson, Emmer, Sanford, & Clements, 1983; Sanford, Emmer, & Clements, 1983). Further work by Evertson and colleagues (Evertson, 1985, 1989; Evertson & Harris, 1999) resulted in a comprehensive teacher training program for classroom management that was selected for the U.S. Department of Education's National Diffusion Network program. Studies on this program indicated its effectiveness in improving student academic performance, teachers' managerial practices, and student behaviors.

Another comprehensive program that incorporates and extends principles from the management research literature has been developed and validated by Freiberg and his associates (Freiberg, 1999; Freiberg, Stein, & Huang, 1995). In addition to emphasizing prevention, their program also focuses on school-wide changes, which includes an emphasis on building a caring climate, and the encouragement of student responsibility through participation in management decisions and functions. Validation of this program has been conducted in inner city schools, where its use has resulted in improved school and classroom climate, student behavior, and academic performance.

In contrast to the aforementioned large-scale studies of classroom management programs, numerous small-scale studies (often dissertation research) have also been done of "packaged" programs such as Assertive Discipline (Canter &

Canter, 1976), whose components have a less secure research base. Results for these latter programs are not particularly supportive, although applications of Reality Therapy (Glasser, 1978) to managing problem behaviors of individual students showed promising results (Emmer & Aussiker, 1990). Research is needed to determine whether updates of some of these programs, such as Glasser's (1990), are effective.

Classroom management research has implications for a number of educational policy matters, such as teacher testing and evaluation, professional development, school reform, and how the public perceives schools. Knowledge of this body of scholarship adds to educational psychologists' ability to contribute constructively to school policy. When short-term, simplistic, or reactive approaches are proposed by policymakers or administrators, we can recommend strategies that are preventive, comprehensive, and sensitive to the realities of the classroom. The short review previously discussed is intended only to sketch some of the main lines of inquiry that have contributed to our current understanding of classroom management. Readers interested in more background will find reviews by Doyle (1986) and Jones (1996) informative.

OTHER RESEARCH WITH IMPLICATIONS FOR CLASSROOM MANAGEMENT AND TEACHER EDUCATION

Research programs that have implications for classroom management have evolved as research in the field has taken a more cognitive slant. These areas of research include the study of teacher cognition—especially development of teaching expertise, affective aspects of teaching and management, and the influence of the classroom context on managerial approaches and strategies.

Teacher Cognition, Expertise, and Classroom Management

Research and writing on teacher cognition and decision making had their genesis approximately 30 years ago as part of the cognitive paradigm shift within psychology. Researchers such as Shavelson and Stern (1981) and Peterson and Clark (1978) examined the interactive nature of teacher decision making within the context of the classroom and investigated the role of teacher thought in how teachers organized and conducted instructional activities. Research on interactive decision making included the examination of how teachers perceived and monitored student behavior, and how their plans were modified when student behavior was perceived as undesirable. Interactive decision making was seen as directly affecting teacher behavior and placed teacher thought as the central causal agent of activity and management in the classroom.

Shavelson and Stern's (1981) model described teacher decision making as the process of integrating knowledge of content, students, and the instructional context to monitor and respond to events in the classroom. Their model implied that classroom management occurs throughout the instructional process and that it is both proactive and reactive in nature. Although later research has depicted teacher thought as even more complex in nature (cf. Calderhead, 1996), the general conclusion from earlier research remains: Teaching is a cognitively challenging process in which teachers are continuously required to make decisions about their instructional and classroom management.

One branch of research on teacher cognition has investigated teacher expertise, usually contrasting the actions and reflections of expert teachers with that of novices. Although the focus of most of these studies primarily has been on instruction, rather than on classroom management, the use of methodologies such as classroom observation (e.g., Leinhardt & Greeno, 1986) and stimulated recall (Peterson & Clark, 1978) also has captured expert teachers' reflections about their classroom management and organization. Pedagogical knowledge of classroom management appears to constitute an essential part of the domain knowledge that expert teachers possess. In contrast, novices appear to be less assured in the specificity and depth of their knowledge about classroom management (Carter, Cushing, Sabers, Stein, & Berliner, 1988).

One of the areas in which expert teachers exhibit more knowledge and skill is the smooth and effective orchestration of their classroom routines and activities. Research on effective classroom managers has established that they spend substantial time and care in establishing and teaching classroom routines and procedures to their students. Novices, in contrast, do not seem to have sufficient ability to use expert-like routines and frequently conduct disorganized lessons (Livingston & Borko, 1989). Berliner (1988) suggested that expert knowledge of routines such as conducting homework reviews, taking attendance, and introducing a lesson, be taught directly to novice teachers

Although expert teachers have well-rehearsed routines that they use in their classrooms, they are also flexible in how they respond to new events that occur in the classroom, and they make instructional decisions in response to these changing factors (Westerman, 1991). Novices, in contrast, tend to teach lessons that are constricted by the plans and objectives that they set for that particular lesson. Livingston and Borko (1989) found that novices had difficulty deviating from scripted lesson plans, which made their instruction vulnerable to student questions and disruptions. Westerman (1991) reported similar rigidity in the classroom instruction of student teachers. A novice teacher in her study reported that she did not want to change the task she had assigned her group of restless students: " ... as I had my lesson plan and I just wanted to get to every part of it and get it finished" (p. 298). Shulman (1987) suggested that this type of inflexibility may be a result of a lack of necessary content knowledge, which limits the ability of the novice to adjust to changing demands in the management of students.

Novices voice more concern about their ability to use management and discipline procedures than do experts (Berliner, 1987). However, during stimulated recall, experienced teachers report a larger percentage of management decisions than do novices during instruction (e.g., Housner & Griffey, 1985). Stough, Palmer, and Leyva (1998) observed that although expert teachers appeared to give little attention to student behavior during classroom observations, in subsequent stimulated recall sessions they frequently referred to the preventive and anticipatory measures that they had taken to avoid behavior and management problems. In contrast, the concern that novices expressed about classroom management was more reactive.

Affective Features of Management

Teaching is full of emotion. Personal histories (cf. Carter & Doyle, 1996) of teachers frequently contain emotional content, and professional writing by teachers sometimes focuses specifically on the topic of emotion and its management. Early research on teacher emotions focused on teaching anxiety and, relatedly, teacher concerns (Keavney & Sinclair, 1978). Much of this research addressed causes and correlates of teacher anxiety, such as discipline and time demands. Some links were found between higher anxiety and lower levels of rapport and job satisfaction. Negative emotion associated with teaching is often related to student behavior, especially when this behavior is disruptive and inappropriate. Teachers report student aggression and behavior that interrupts class activities to be the most common stressors, with anger and depression being typical emotional reactions (Blase, 1986). Schonfeld (1992) found that beginning teachers in school environments that contained higher perceived levels of student behaviors such as threats or confrontations, and that included chronic stressors such as unmotivated students or overcrowded classes, experienced more depressive symptoms than beginning teachers in less stressful settings. A longitudinal study of teacher burnout in the Netherlands (Brouwers & Tomic, 2000) found that depersonalization and feelings of a lack of accomplishment (associated with burnout) were preceded by low efficacy beliefs in classroom management, and emotional exhaustion led to lower efficacy in classroom management.

Attributions teachers make about the basis for student behavior provides some insight into the causes of teacher emotions. Teachers are likely to feel anger and to endorse punitive or rejecting strategies when student misbehavior is seen as intentional and controllable (Brophy & McCaslin, 1992). Teachers also tend to respond with anger or frustration when they perceive that students fail because of a lack of effort, but they feel pity when they attribute failure to low ability (Stough, Palmer, & Leyva, 1998; Weiner & Graham, 1984). Teachers feel pride when students succeed through effort, but feel guilt when students give up (Prawat, Byers, & Anderson, 1983). One study (Emmer, 1994) reported that middle school teachers' negative emotionality was more intense in response to behavior problems than to poor student performance. The probable reason for the difference was that teachers believed that the misbehaviors were more controllable, whereas the bases for poor student performance were attributable to multiple sources and were viewed as less controllable by the teacher.

Naturalistic studies of teachers identify emotions as a key influence on teachers' interpretations of their own and their students' actions and on teachers' subsequent instructional and managerial strategies. For example, Hargreaves and Tucker (1991) analyzed the emotional response of guilt in teachers, illustrating its causes and consequences. They concluded that guilt results from conflicts among several factors: teachers' commitment to nurture children, the ambiguity inherent in determining teachers' effects on their students, increasing demands for accountability, and unrealistically high expectations. If not managed properly, the consequences of guilt are resentment, burnout, and cynicism. Escaping guilt traps, according to Hargreaves and Tucker, requires achieving a realistic balance of the various demands, receiving collaborative support from colleagues, and easing accountability pressures. Stough and Emmer (1998) found that beginning teachers whose students reacted with hostility during test feedback activities experienced negative emotions such as frustration and anger. Subsequently, some teachers altered their classroom management strategies by adopting highly structured feedback approaches to control student interactions, even though these strategies greatly limited opportunities for discussion and the teachers had earlier indicated that they believed discussion would help students gain a deeper comprehension of the content.

We believe that relations among teacher emotion, classroom management, and teaching practice are important to understand and need additional research. The effects of teacher emotion on burnout, teacher decision making, and behavior make the topic appropriate for inclusion in the teacher education curriculum. In addition to educational psychology content on child and adolescent emotional development, for example, curricular activities focused on teachers' acquiring an understanding of their reactions to student behavior, and of the coping processes they use to manage it, would be useful.

THE INFLUENCE OF CONTEXT ON CLASSROOM MANAGEMENT

Many types of teaching contexts are possible to identify, with important implications for management. Teaching contexts may vary according to instructional goals, subject matter taught, grade or age and other student characteristics, use of technology, and so forth. For example, school and classroom settings having students from predominately lower or working class backgrounds are more challenging because students have been found to be less inclined to cooperate with teachers (Metz, 1993). Classrooms whose students have emotional or behavior disorders may require a combination of high levels of structure, teacher caring, and curricular adaptation (Cambone, 1994). Some management concepts and propositions, however, seem to transcend most contexts and thus may be regarded as general. For example, Kounin's (1970) concept of withitness would appear to be important in any teaching context.

Although there are many contexts that might cause some variation in management characteristics, we consider two contexts that are sufficiently widespread to warrant special attention to their implications for classroom management: the inclusion classroom and cooperative learning activities.

The Inclusion Context

The Individuals with Disabilities Education Act of 1990 mandates that students with disabilities be provided an appropriate education in the least restrictive environment, which, for most students, is the general education classroom. Although there is controversy about the inclusive education movement, general classroom teachers are increasingly placed in inclusive classrooms that contain students with a wide range of instructional needs (Tomlinson et al., 1997). In addition to challenges faced by the general educator in teaching students with special needs, special educators now play an expanded role, providing classroom instruction, consulting or coteaching with other educators, coordinating educational services with other health and human service agencies, and monitoring related services, such as speech therapy. These changes, as a consequence, will influence the management competencies required of both general educators and special educators.

There are few studies on the management strategies of teachers who instruct inclusive classrooms, and most of them highlight the limitations that teachers exhibit in this area. For example, McIntosh (1994) reported that during whole-class instruction, teachers make few adaptations to meet the individual learning needs of special education students. Teachers appear to lack the training and background required to effectively instruct students with disabilities. A 1992 survey conducted by Schumm and Vaughn (1992) found that although 98% of general educators rated their knowledge and skills in planning for general education students as "excellent" or "good," only 39% gave a high rating to their planning for special education students. Teachers also express a high level of concern with behavioral problems occurring while instructing students with special needs (Blanton, Blanton, & Cross, 1993; Hanrahan, Goodman, & Rapagna, 1990), but research on the effective management of these behaviors within the context of the inclusive classroom is lacking.

Noting that many students with special needs seem to require direct instruction of appropriate behaviors, some researchers (Carpenter & McKee-Higgins, 1996; Colvin, Kameenui, & Sugai, 1993) suggested what they term an *instructional approach* to behavior management. In this approach, the focus is on directly instructing students in appropriate behaviors and responses to classroom situations and activities. Similarly, other research (e.g., Rademacher, Schumaker, & Deshler, 1996) suggested that teachers improve the quality and level of challenge of assignments given to students with mild disabilities to increase student engagement—and thereby decrease off-task and disruptive behaviors. These interventions are not novel approaches to classroom management, rather they promote classic techniques such as developing classroom rules, establishing routines and procedures, and raising the academic expectations of students.

Applied behavior analysis is also used to manage specific behaviors of students. Educational psychologists long have had a love–hate relation with applied behavior analysis. On the one hand, for many years, it was one of the few areas in psychology that could directly address the beginning teacher's concerns about discipline. Well into the 70s, it was the primary source for classroom management content in educational psychology texts. On the other hand, many educational psychologists have found fault with using extrinsic reinforcement in classrooms, and the behaviorists' limited concern for the role of cognition has swum against the philosophic current in recent decades. The emphasis on preventive management strategies also has deflected attention from the management of specific problem behaviors. Teachers, however, may need to implement individualized discipline plans for some included students, and the use of behavior analysis to assist in management through the control of antecedents and consequences may be a necessary component in the management of individual students who do not respond to traditional group-based instructional techniques.

A significant recent advance in applied behavior analysis has been the refinement of functional analysis, which attempts to examine systematically a problem behavior's function as well as the motivation for the behavior (e.g., Mace, Lalli, & Lalli, 1991; O'Neill et al., 1997). Through examining the environmental factors that evoke and maintain problem behaviors, the "function" or motivation of a targeted behavior is determined and the intervention or instructional accommodation is subsequently designed. Single-case research designs allow for the empirical analysis of these individualized treatments.

Although group-based management strategies are likely to remain a mainstay in the preparation of teachers, educational psychologists should expand their repertoire to adequately prepare regular teachers to deal with the unique challenges of students with disabilities.

Cooperative Learning Activities

Cooperative learning groups are another context which may require modification of recommended management strategies. Some common elements of the various cooperative learning models can be identified: group goals or task interdependence, some form of individual accountability, and good group interaction. Numerous literature reviews and metaanalyses support the use of cooperative groups on a variety of academic tasks (e.g., Qin, Johnson, & Johnson, 1995, for evidence on problem solving). Compared to formats that require students to "sit and watch" or that rely extensively on individual seatwork activities, group formats offer greater potential for participation, feedback, and interactive construction of meaning. The instructional model underlying traditional teacher-paced activities is one of "transmission of knowledge," whereas the premise for cooperative learning programs is social construction of understanding and participation in a learning community (Brophy, 1999). Several classroom researchers (Cohen, 1994; Freiberg, 1999) noted the potential for inconsistency between the instructional goals and methods of cooperative learning and teacher-centered management systems. Attempts to adhere to strict limits, for example, on student talk and movement during instructional activities, would be counter to the need for discussion and group investigation that many cooperative activities require. Some traditional management functions are likely to continue to be relevant, with appropriate modifications: for example, monitoring students in groups, establishing classroom routines, and teaching desirable group behaviors. Some new management skills also may be needed, such as keeping students accountable for individual work in a group context, helping students learn to seek explanations from and to give feedback to other students, or pacing groups working at different rates or different tasks. Some forms of cooperative learning utilize multiple types of grouping arrangements and emphasize affective outcomes as well as academic outcomes (Johnson & Johnson, 1999), thus increasing the complexity of management. Most teachers who adopt cooperative learning do shift their role from director to facilitator of student learning (Antil, Jenkins, Wayne, & Vadasy, 1998), although some teachers prefer to retain considerable control over the structure of these classroom activities (Emmer & Gerwels, 1998).

When cooperative learning groups are used, teachers continue to be active managers, but the focus shifts to helping students learn the behaviors necessary to work effectively in groups whose goal is the active construction of meaning. It is important to realize that most classrooms that utilize cooperative learning will continue to use a combination of formats for instruction, not just the grouping of students. Consequently, the task of learning about management is more complex for the novice teacher who is beginning to use these new formats while mastering traditional ones.

CLASSROOM MANAGEMENT AND TEACHER EDUCATION

Classroom management research by educational psychologists has contributed substantially to our understanding of effective classroom practice. This body of research, moreover, along with other classroom-based research; has increased the relevance of educational psychology for teacher education and teacher educators. The emphasis in this body of research on careful observation, description, and measurement has helped produce results that can be translated into effective action plans for teachers. Increased availability of knowledge about classrooms has resulted in more applicable content for teacher education. Twenty to 30 years ago very little research-based information about management, other than that extracted from applied behavior analysis, could be found in basic educational psychology textbooks. Books devoted to classroom management were nonexistent. Currently, most texts in educational psychology contain a chapter or two that present basic concepts, many of which provide a solid conceptual overview (e.g., Borich & Tombari, 1997; Good & Brophy, 1997; Woolfolk, 1998), and there are many management texts from which to choose. Thus, students whose teacher education programs include a survey course in educational psychology will have had at least an introduction to the declarative knowledge in the field. In addition, according to a survey by Wesley and Vocke (1992, cited in Jones, 1996), in a solid minority of teacher education programs (37%), students take a course in classroom management.

The Development of Classroom Management Knowledge

As with other aspects of teaching expertise, the development of classroom management understanding and skill is likely to be a staged process, acquired over many years (Berliner, 1988), and be characterized by discontinuities, especially as the teacher encounters new teaching contexts (Bullough & Baughman, 1995; Cambone, 1994). In addition, beginning teachers' perspectives on classrooms are often incomplete and idiosyncratic, and rapidly reorganize their pedagogical knowledge during student teaching (Jones & Vesilund, 1996). Knowledge of effective classroom management should therefore include adequate conceptualization (Brophy, 1999; Doyle, 1990), rather than being learned as discrete concepts and skills, and should give developing teachers a research-based heuristic for examining and formulating their views on management. Neither should this knowledge be separated from practice, as it has been found that didactic components, separated from the situations in which they have application, are not very effective in teacher education (Wideen, Mayer-Smith, & Moon; 1998). Developing understanding about classroom management thus requires experience in classroom contexts to be pragmatic; that is, to be integrated into the network of scripts, expectations, and routines that the teacher will utilize in the classroom and to result in the effective management of students.

Methods that promote the reflective-practioner approach to teacher education attempt to situate classroom management within real-world contexts and events. Videotapes of classroom management situations may illustrate varied contexts and provide opportunities for analysis. Alternate forms of teaching classroom management skills and increasing management self-efficacy have included microcomputer simulations (e.g., Murphy, Kauffman, & Strang; 1987) and video-aided programs (e.g., Hagen, Gutkin, Wilson, & Oats, 1998; Overbaugh, 1995). The use of cases in teacher education has been rediscovered as a means of providing varied contexts and opportunities for constructing understanding about teaching and about management (Meserth, 1996; Shulman, 1986). Case-based instruction also has the advantage of providing novice teachers with rich, contextualized descriptions of classrooms and behavioral problems, while eliminating some of the complexity and immediacy of the classroom that can create difficulties for novice learning (Sykes & Bird, 1992).

An increasingly popular design for incorporating early field experiences and coordinating its components with teacher education curriculum is the Professional Development School (PDS) model. Increased exposure to classrooms and students in the PDS model also increases the encounters that novice teachers have with classroom management. Components that make use of classroom experiences such as journal writing, reflective activities, and portfolios can enhance classroom management competence in the field-based PDS, in addition to those mentioned previously. Because PDS students are usually in a cohort, taking the same classes and teaching in the same schools, this context can also provide a supportive teacher network or community (Lieberman, 2000) that is organized around learning how to teach and how to manage classrooms.

SUMMARY

Smith and Rivera (1995) pointed out that as classrooms become more diverse in nature, the need for classroom management techniques that can be used with both individuals and groups of students becomes more critical. Educational psychology has contributed substantially to the research base for this important area of pedagogical content knowledge and practice. Research on teacher thinking and on affective aspects of management has deepened our awareness of the challenging and complex nature of teaching's managerial dimensions. Varied teaching contexts, such as cooperative learning or inclusion settings, highlight the need for flexible and effective management skills. Educational psychologists can continue to contribute to the field of teacher education by incorporating relevant classroom management content into their courses, by cooperating with teacher education colleagues to plan for managerial content across the curriculum, by including experiential components that take place in different classroom contexts and highlighting their managerial features, and by encouraging through reflection the construction of understanding about this crucial topic.

REFERENCES

Allen, J. D. (1986). Classroom management: Students' perspectives, goals, and strategies. *American Educational Research Journal, 23*, 437–459.

Anderson, L., Evertson, C., & Brophy, J. (1979). An experimental study of effective teaching in first grade reading groups. *Elementary School Journal, 79*, 193–223.

Anderson, L., Evertson, C., & Emmer, E. (1980). Dimensions in classroom management derived from recent research. *Journal of Curriculum Studies, 12*, 343–356.

Antil, L, Jenkins, J., Wayne, S., & Vadasy, P. (1998). Cooperative learning: Prevalence, conceptualizations, and the relation between research and practice. *American Educational Research Journal, 35*, 419–454.

Arlin, M. (1979). Teacher transitions can interrupt time flow in classrooms. *American Educational Research Journal, 16*, 42–56.

Berliner, D. C. (1987). Ways of thinking about students and classrooms by more and less experienced teachers. In J. Calderhead (Ed.), *Exploring teachers' thinking* (pp. 60–83). London: Cassell.

Berliner, D. C. (1988). The development of expertise in pedagogy. *Charles W. Hunt Memorial Lecture*. New Orleans, LA: AACTE.

Blanton, W., Blanton, L., & Cross, L. (1993, April). *An exploratory study of how expert and novice regular education teachers and special education teachers think and make instructional decisions about special needs students*. Paper presented at the meeting of the American Education Research Association, Atlanta, GA.

Blase, J. J. (1986). A qualitative analysis of sources of teacher stress. *American Educational Research Journal, 23*, 13–40.

Borich, G., & Tombari, M. (1997). *Educational psychology: A contemporary approach* (2nd ed.). New York: Longman.

Brophy, J. (1999). Perspectives of classroom management. In H. J. Freiberg (Ed.), *Beyond behaviorism: Changing the classroom management paradigm* (pp. 43–56). Boston: Allyn & Bacon.

Brophy, J., & Evertson, C. (1976). *Learning from teaching: a developmental perspective.* Boston: Allyn and Bacon.

Brophy, J., & McCaslin, M. (1992). Teachers' reports of how they perceive and cope with problem students. *Elementary School Journal, 93*, 3–68.

Brouwers, A., & Tomic, W. (2000). A longitudinal study of teacher burnout and perceived self-efficacy in classroom management. *Teaching and Teacher Education, 16*, 239–254.

Bullough, R. V., & Baughman, K. (1995). Changing contexts and expertise in teaching: First-year teacher after seven years. *Teaching and Teacher Education, 11*, 461–477.

Calderhead, J. (1996). Teachers: Beliefs and knowledge. In D. Berliner and R. Calfee (Eds.), *Handbook of educational psychology* (pp. 709–725). New York: Simon & Schuster.

Cambone, J. (1994). *Teaching troubled children*. New York: Teachers College Press.

Canter, L., & Canter, M. (1976). *Assertive discipline: A take-charge approach for today's educator*. Santa Monica, CA: Lee Canter and Associates.

Carpenter, S. L., & McKee-Higgins, E. (1996). Behavior management in inclusive classrooms. *Remedial and Special Education, 17*(4), 195–203.

Carter, K., Cushing, K., Sabers, D., Stein, P., & Berliner, D. (1988). Expert–novice differences in perceiving and processing visual classroom stimuli. *Journal of Teacher Education, 39*(3), 25–31.

Carter, K., & Doyle, W. (1996). Personal narrative and life history in learning to teach. In J. Sikula (Ed.), *Handbook of research on teacher education* (2nd ed., pp. 120–142). New York: Simon & Schuster.

Cohen, E. G. (1994). *Designing groupwork: Strategies for the heterogeneous classroom* (2nd ed.). New York: Teachers College Press.

Colvin, G., Kameenui, E. J., & Sugai, G. (1993). Reconceptualizing behavior management and school-wide discipline in general education. *Education and Treatment of Children, 16,* 193–201.

Council for Exceptional Children (1998). What every special educator must know: The international standards for the preparation and licensure of special educators. Reston, VA: Council for Exceptional Children.

Doyle, W. (1986). Classroom organization and management. In M. Wittrock (Ed.), *Handbook of Research on Teaching* (3rd ed., pp. 392–431). New York: Macmillan.

Doyle, W. (1990). Classroom knowledge as a foundation for teaching. *Teachers College Record, 91,* 347–360.

Duke, D. (Ed.). (1979). *Classroom management: The 78th yearbook of the National Society for the Study of Education, Part II.* Chicago: University of Chicago Press.

Emmer, E. (1994, April). *Teacher emotions and classroom management.* Paper presented at the annual meeting of the American Educational Research Association, New Orleans, LA.

Emmer, E., & Aussiker, A. (1990). School and classroom discipline programs: How well do they work? In O. C. Moles (Ed.), *Student discipline strategies: Research and practice* (pp. 129–166). Albany, NY: SUNY Press.

Emmer, E., Evertson, C., & Anderson, L. (1980). Effective management at the beginning of the school year. *Elementary School Journal, 80,* 219–231.

Emmer, E., & Gerwels, M. (1998, April). *Teachers' views and uses of cooperative learning.* Paper presented at the annual meeting of the American Educational Research Association, San Diego, CA.

Evertson, C. M. (1985). Training teachers in classroom management: An experiment in secondary classrooms. *Journal of Educational Research, 79,* 51–58.

Evertson, C. M. (1989). Improving elementary classroom management: A school based training program for beginning the year. *Journal of Educational Research, 83,* 82–90.

Evertson C. M., & Emmer E. T. (1982). Effective management at the beginning of the year in junior high classes. *Journal of Educational Psychology 74,* 485–498.

Evertson, C., Emmer, E., Sanford, J., & Clements, B. (1983). Improving classroom management: An experiment in elementary classrooms. *Elementary School Journal, 84,* 173–188.

Evertson, C., & Harris, A.(1999). Support for managing learning-centered classrooms: The Classroom Organization and Management Program. In H. J. Freiberg (Ed.), *Beyond behaviorism: Changing the classroom management paradigm* (pp. 59–74). Boston: Allyn & Bacon.

Evertson, C., Sanford, J., & Emmer, E. (1981). Effects of class heterogeneity in junior high school. *American Educational Research Journal, 18,* 219–232.

Freiberg, H. J. (Ed.). (1999). *Beyond behaviorism: Changing the classroom management paradigm.* Boston: Allyn & Bacon.

Freiberg, H. J., Stein, T. A., & Huang, S. (1995). The effects of classroom management intervention on student achievement in inner-city elementary schools. *Educational Research and Evaluation, 1,* 33–66.

Glasser, W. (1978). Disorder in our schools: Causes and remedies. *Phi Delta Kappan, 59,* 322–325.

Glasser, W. (1990). *The quality school: Managing students without coercion.* New York: Perennial Library.

Good, T., & Brophy, J. (1997). *Looking in classrooms.* New York: Longman.

Good, T., & Grouws, D. (1977). Teaching effects: A process–product study in fourth grade mathematics classrooms. *Journal of Teacher Education, 28*(3), 49–54.

Hagen, K. M., Gutkin, T. B., Wilson, C. P., & Oats, R. G. (1998). Using vicarious experience and verbal persuasion to enhance self-efficacy in pre-service teachers: "Priming the Pump" for consultation. *School Psychology Quarterly, 13,* 169–178.

Hanrahan, J., Goodman, W., & Rapagna, S. (1990). Preparing mentally retarded students for mainstreaming: Priorities of regular class and special school teachers. *American Journal on Mental Retardation, 94,* 470–474.

Hargreaves, A., & Tucker, E. (1991). Teaching and guilt: Exploring the feelings of teaching. *Teaching and Teacher Education, 7,* 491–505.

Housner, L. D., & Griffey, D. C. (1985). Teacher cognition: Difference in planning and interactive decision making between experienced and inexperienced teachers. *Research Quarterly for Exercise and Sport, 56,* 45–53.

Jackson, P. W. (1968). *Life in classrooms.* New York: Holt, Rinehart & Winston.

Jacob, E. (1987). Qualitative research traditions: A review. *Review of Educational Research, 57,* 1–50.

Johnson, D. W., & Johnson, R. T. (1999). The three Cs of school and classroom management. In H. J. Freiberg (Ed.), *Beyond behaviorism: Changing the classroom management paradigm* (pp. 119–144). Boston: Allyn & Bacon.

Jones, V. (1996). Classroom management. In J. Sikula (Ed.), *Handbook of research on teacher education* (2nd ed., pp. 503–521). New York: Simon & Schuster.

Jones, M. G., & Vesilund, E. M. (1996). Putting practice into theory: Changes in the organization of preservice teachers' pedagogical knowledge. *American Educational Research Journal, 33,* 91–117.

Keavney, G., & Sinclair, K. E. (1978). Teacher concerns and teacher anxiety: A neglected topic of classroom research. *Review of Educational Research. 48,* 273–290.

Kounin, J. S. (1970). *Discipline and group management in classrooms.* New York: Holt, Rinehart & Winston.

Kounin, J. S., & Obradovic, L. (1968). Managing emotional disturbed children in regular classrooms: A replication and extension. *Journal of Special Education, 2,* 1–13.

Lambert, N. M. (1994). Seating arrangements in classrooms. *The International Encyclopedia of Education (2nd ed.), 9,* 5355–5359.

Leinhardt, G., & Greeno, J. (1986). The cognitive skill of teaching. *Journal of Educational Psychology, 78,* 75–95.

Lieberman, A. (2000). Networks as learning communities: Shaping the future of teacher development. *Journal of Teacher Education, 51,* 221–227.

Livingston, C., & Borko, H. (1989). Cognition and improvisation: Differences in mathematics instruction by expert and novice teachers. *American Educational Research Journal, 26,* 473–498.

Mace, F. C., Lalli, J. S., & Lalli, E. P. (1991). Functional analysis and treatment of aberrant behavior. *Research in Developmental Disabilities, 12,* 155–180.

McCaslin, M., & Good, T. L. (1992). Compliant cognition: The misalliance of management and instructional goals in current school reform. *Educational Researcher, 21*(2), 4–17.

McCaslin, M., & Good, T. L. (1998). Moving beyond management as sheer compliance: Helping students to develop goal coordination strategies. *Educational Horizons, 76,* 169–176.

McIntosh, R. (1994). Observations of students with learning disabilities in general education classrooms. *Exceptional Children, 60,* 249–261.

Meserth, K. (1996). Cases and case methods in teacher education. In J. Sikula (Ed.), *Handbook of research on teacher education* (2nd ed., pp. 722–744). New York: Simon & Schuster.

Murphy, D. M., Kauffman, J. M., & Strang, H. R. (1987). Using microcomputer simulation to teach classroom management skills to preservice teachers. *Behavioral Disorders, 13,* 20–34.

Metz, M. H. (1993). Teachers' ultimate dependence on their students. In J. W. Little and M. W. McLaughlin (Eds.), *Teachers' work: Individuals, colleagues, and contexts* (pp. 104–136). New York: Teachers College Press.

O'Neill, R., Horner, R., Albin, R., Sprague, J., Storey, K., & Newton, J. S. (1997). *Functional analysis and program development for problem behavior* (2nd ed.). Pacific Grove, CA: Brooks/Cole.

Overbaugh, R. C. (1995). The efficacy of interactive video for teaching basic classroom management skills to pre-service teachers. *Computers in Human Behavior, 11*, 511–527.

Peterson, P. L., & Clark, C. M. (1978). Teachers' reports of their cognitive processes during teaching. *American Educational Research Journal, 15*, 555–565.

Prawat, R. S., Byers, J. S., & Anderson, A. H. (1983). An attributional analysis of teachers' affective reactions to student success and failure. *American Educational Research Journal, 20*, 137–152.

Qin, Z., Johnson, D., & Johnson, R. (1995). Cooperative versus competitive efforts and problem solving. *Review of Educational Research, 65*, 129–144.

Rademacher, J. A., Schumaker, J. B., & Deshler, D. D. (1996). Development and validation of a classroom assignment routine for inclusive settings. *Learning Disability Quarterly, 19,* 163–177.

Sanford, J., Emmer, E., & Clements, B. (1983). Improving classroom management. *Educational Leadership, 40*(7), 56–60.

Sanford, J., & Evertson, C. (1981). Classroom management in a low SES junior high: Three case studies. *Journal of Teacher Education, 32*(1), 34–38.

Schonfeld, I. S. (1992). A longitudinal study of occupational stressors and depressive symptoms in first-year female teachers. *Teaching and Teacher Education, 8*, 151–158.

Schumm, J. S., & Vaughn, S. (1992). Planning for mainstreamed special education students: Perceptions of general classroom teachers. *Exceptionality, 3*, 81–90.

Shavelson, R. J., & Stern, P. (1981). Research on teachers' pedagogical thoughts, judgments, decisions, and behavior. *Review of Educational Research, 51*, 455–498.

Shulman, L. S. (1986). Those who understand: Knowledge growth in teaching. *Educational Researcher, 15*(2), 4–14.

Shulman, L. S. (1987). Knowledge and teaching: Foundations of the new reform. *Harvard Educational Review, 57*, 1–22.

Smith, D. D., & Rivera, D. P. (1995). Discipline in special education and general education settings. *Focus on Exceptional Children, 27*(5), 1–14.

Soar, R., & Soar, R. (1979). Emotional climate and management. In P. Peterson & H. Walberg (Eds.), *Research on teaching: Concepts, findings, and implications* (pp. 97–119). Berkeley, CA: McCutchan.

Stough, L., & Emmer, E. (1998). Teacher emotions and test feedback. *International Journal of Qualitative Studies in Education, 11*, 341–362.

Stough, L. M., Palmer, D. P., & Leyva, C. (1998, February). *Listening to voices of experience in special education.* Paper presented at the meeting of the American Educational Research Association, San Diego, CA.

Sykes, G., & Bird, T. (1992). Teacher education and the case idea. *Review of Research in Education, 18*, 457–521.

Tomlinson, C. A., Callahan, C. M., Tomchin, E. M., Eiss, N., Imbeau, M., & Landrum, M. (1997). Becoming architects of communities of learning: Addressing academic diversity in contemporary classrooms. *Exceptional Children, 63*, 269–282.

Weiner, B., & Graham, S. (1984). An attributional approach to emotional development. In C. Izard, J. Kagan, & R. Zajonc (Eds.), *Emotions, cognition, and behavior* (pp. 121–135). Cambridge, MA: Harvard University Press.

Wesley, D., & Vocke, D. (1992, February). *Classroom discipline and teacher education.* Paper presented at the annual meeting of the Association of Teacher Educators, Orlando, FL.

Westerman, D. A. (1991). Expert and novice teacher decision making. *Journal of Teacher Education, 42*(4), 292–305.

Wideen, M., Mayer-Smith, J., & Moon, B. (1998). A critical analysis of the research on learning to teach: Making the case for an ecological perspective on inquiry. *Review of Educational Research, 68*, 130–178.

Woolfolk, A. (1998). *Educational psychology* (7th ed.). Boston: Allyn & Bacon.

EDUCATIONAL PSYCHOLOGIST, *36*(2), 113–126

Expectancy Effects in the Classroom: A Special Focus on Improving the Reading Performance of Minority Students in First-Grade Classrooms

Thomas L. Good and Sharon L. Nichols
Department of Educational Psychology
University of Arizona

Teacher expectations for students has been an exciting topic of research in educational psychology since the publication of *Pygmalion in the Classroom* by Robert Rosenthal and Lenore Jacobson (1968). This article reviews the development of research in this area and notes the rich application value of this literature for social policy issues. The article discusses an intervention program for improving the reading performance of 1st-grade low income minority students in general (and Black low income students specifically). This example is but 1 instance of how this broad research base could be used to improve performance in various social settings.

Educational psychologists have long researched the relation between teachers' expectations and student performance. Teacher expectations are inferences (based on prior experiences or information) about the level of student performance that is likely to occur in the future (Brophy & Good, 1970; Good & Brophy, 2000). Teachers' expectations, like expectations in other social settings, tend to be self-sustaining because expectations may affect perception, causing some teachers to be more likely to see what they expect and less likely to notice the unexpected. Further, teachers' continuing interpretations of ambiguous classroom behavior may consistently operate in ways that confirm their original expectations. In turn, teacher expectations may affect student performance because teachers decide what students are assigned to learn and judge how well they do.

Teachers' expectations not only may influence teacher behavior, but also students' expectancies and behaviors. Students' expectations are formed by social performance comparisons made by themselves and their teachers and by their own beliefs of personal ability as well as those of their teachers and parents. Some students are more likely to be influenced by teacher beliefs than others (see Weinstein & McKown, 1998).

Requests for reprints should be sent to Thomas L. Good, Department of Educational Psychology, University of Arizona, P.O. Box 210069, Tucson, AZ 85721. E-mail: tgood@mail.ed.arizona.edu

Expectation effects are widely evident in the popular culture. For example, two Academy Award-winning films focused on the power of "expectation effects" as their central plot—one on negative expectation effects and the other on positive ones. In the classic movie "Gaslight," Ingrid Bergman brilliantly portrays the role of a vivacious intelligent woman who systematically comes to question her sanity because of the consistent and vicious communication of low expectations from the film's villain (Charles Boyer). In contrast, in "My Fair Lady," Audrey Hepburn skillfully portrays the uneducated flower girl who is dramatically transformed by the professor's (Rex Harrison) consistent communication of positive expectations (and the hard work of both individuals). Further, Jack Nicholson brilliantly illustrates how ambiguous behavior is subjected to multiple interpretations in "One Flew Over the Cuckoo's Nest." Or, to take an example from literature, consider the words of Tolstoy's Prince Andrey: "We lost because we told ourselves we lost." (Berlin, 1953, p. 54).

In contrast to movies and literature, reality is both more complex and more difficult to represent in a single story. In real life, the negative expectations of the "villain" and the positive expectations of the "teacher" do not always impact another's behavior in dramatic ways. Indeed, the difficulty of illustrating the effects of teacher expectations in research have led some academics to contend that expectation research is more fiction than reality. For example, Wineburg (1987) suggested that expectation research was overblown. Although not a researcher in the area, Wineburg argued, for example, that the field has been counterproductive by its suggesting "that the central, if not the entire, cause of school failure resides in the minds of teachers" (p. 35).

We comment on Wineburg's (1987) review in this introduction because he represents a prototype of the problems that occur when the work of psychology is analyzed in secondary and tertiary sources (as Good & Levin, 2001, noted in the introduction of this special issue). No active researcher we know of in the area has made the claim that the central cause of school failure is low teacher expectations.[1] Indeed, from the beginning of research on teacher expectation effects (Brophy & Good, 1970; Good, 1970; Rosenthal & Jacobson, 1968) and through to today (Ferguson 1998a, 1998b), expectation scholars suggest that expectations are but one of the many factors that may in some cases contribute to lower student performance.

PURPOSE

In this article, we address three goals. First, we locate psychologists and educational psychologists in this historical paradigm by illustrating some of the key points that have emerged from the expectation research literature. In doing so, we discuss an emerging area of inquiry and contend that teachers' conceptions of students both as learners and social beings (and students' mediation of these teachers' beliefs and behavior) are more powerful ways to conceptualize the impact of teacher expectations rather than simply exploring teachers' beliefs about student ability or social characteristics. Second, we illustrate the power of this conception by discussing the critical importance of first grade for students from low income homes—especially Black students from low income homes. Third, we propose a general intervention plan—grounded in expectation theory—that focuses on first graders and the systematic reduction of short- and long-term racial achievement differences found at this level and subsequently. This analysis is especially relevant now that researchers are once again actively exploring ethnic difference in students' test scores (see Jencks & Phillips, 1998).

Teacher Beliefs are Potentially Powerful: Some Background

Although the literature on teacher expectancy effects in the classroom is considerably more complex than simply "a belief" in the teacher's mind, it is important to understand just how powerful such beliefs can be. Building on a Vygotskian theoretical approach to classroom learning (Vygotsky, 1962), it is clear that teachers inevitably make decisions about how much structure to provide students and the types of learning challenges that students can conquer. Some teachers provide low-achieving students too much structure and others too little. These decisions ultimately relate to perceptions of present ability and one's potential to grow as a learner. For example, in the early grades, teachers decide what the child will read and with whom he or she will read. Further, the teacher grades the quality of the child's work. Teachers' beliefs about first-grade reading assignments and how to teach top and bottom groups have shown to have powerful impact on students' performance in some cases (Eder, 1981; Weinstein, 1976). First-grade teachers do more than create reading groups: They also decide who will be first in line and who will greet visitors on behalf of the class. These are not insignificant events in the lives of children as these decisions convey status and respect. Teachers make decisions about students both as academic learners and social beings (McCaslin & Good, 1996).

Difficulty of Establishing Teacher Effects

Understanding learning in school settings is difficult. Unlike laboratory situations in which students can be shielded from much of their past learning history (e.g., anxiety about a teacher watching them perform, wondering if peers will laugh at the response they're about to make because they often do), in naturalistic and field experiments in classrooms, a student's history as a learner is a concomitant factor of success or failure. Students do not start first grade evenly. Some are reading at advanced levels and have extensive vocabularies; other students do not know the alphabet. Some students have learned to answer adult "questions" at home; other students have learned that adults do not ask questions to which they know the answer (e.g., What color is your truck?) and hence are baffled when teachers ask questions to which "answers" are obvious (Heath, 1983). Some students enter first-grade classrooms well-rested and replete with enthusiasm; others enter the same classrooms hungry and fatigued. Some enter classrooms that are modern and replete with resources including high-quality teachers and state of the art technology; others enter classrooms lacking in basic resources such as leak-proof ceilings and chalk—let alone modern computers.

It is well known that, on average, students who enter first grade behind other students never catch up with their more advantaged peers (Entwisle, Alexander, & Olson, 1997). This is not another attack on the "ineffectiveness" of schooling as without formal schooling, the gap between more and less advantaged learners would likely widen dramatically over time. Even critics who once challenged the power of schools to impact students' achievement (Jencks, 1972) have come to accept the fact that schools are critically important in preventing the achievement gap from widening (Jencks, 1978).

Aside from this important problem (students on average do not catch up), there is also clear knowledge that individual students make more or less progress. Some disadvantaged students close or narrow the gap; others do not. The field of research on teacher expectation effects has been a rich source of theory, research, and debate about the type of classroom environments that facilitate the achievement of students who enter the classroom at a disadvantage—and it continues to be

[1]However, we agree with Wineburg (1987) that policy makers and the media misused these findings.

a solid area of research (Brophy, 1998; Ferguson, 1998a, 1998b). This research is replete with arguments about the size of expectation effects, including when they are likely to occur, how they can be measured, and what types of research are recommended for future work (see Good & Thompson, 1998; Jussim, Smith, Madon, & Palumbo, 1998; Weinstein & McKown, 1998).

IDEAS AND FINDINGS FROM EXPECTATION RESEARCH

Research on teacher expectations for the past 30-plus years has represented an active area of theory and methodological debate. The findings and implications from this research for classrooms and schools are considerable (extensive reviews of this research can be found in many sources, including Brophy, 1998; Good & Brophy, 2000; & Weinstein & McKown, 1998). Here, we do not review the literature systematically, but illustrate for students of educational psychology and other interested readers some of the nuances over time that have shaped a different understanding of expectation effects.

Brief Historical Context

For 30 years it has been known that some teachers differentially interact with students they believe to be more and less capable (Brophy & Good, 1970; Good, 1969; Hoehn, 1954) on the basis of the affect they hold toward them (Silberman, 1969), and on the basis of student race (Katz, 1972; Leacock, 1969), student social class (Davis & Dollard, 1940; Smith, 1965), and student gender (Hess, Shipman, Brophy, & Bear, 1969; Lippitt & Gold, 1959; Meyer & Thompson, 1956;). Furthermore, students are more than any single characteristic (e.g., achievement or gender) and there are compelling data to illustrate, for example, that low-achieving male and female students receive different treatments from teachers in the same classroom (Good, Sikes, & Brophy, 1973).

Research on Teacher Expectations in the Classroom

The debate on self-fulfilling prophecies has long been discussed in the social (Merton, 1948) and psychological sciences (Clark, 1963). However, the research impetus for examining the phenomenon was largely stimulated by numerous laboratory studies by social psychologists who illustrated unequivocally that the provision of false information about others (e.g., their sociability, their intelligence) could influence how others perceived and behaved. These results were exciting in part because in the late 1960s and 1970s social scientists and policymakers were beginning to argue strongly for the power of the environment in impacting human performance and learning.

Rosenthal (1985) provided a thorough review of early research on expectancies including Ebbinghaus's (1885/1913) observation that early trials in an experiment can be a cause of self-fulfilling prophecies and Rice's (1929) classic study of how researchers' beliefs influenced interview responses about the causes of poverty. His review also contains more recent research examples from the 1960s and 1970s. However, what sparked large-scale research interest in the self-fulfilling prophecy notion was the publication of Rosenthal and Jacobson's *Pygmalion in the Classroom* (1968). This work was controversial and debated by many who both believed and did not believe the original results (Elashoff & Snow, 1971), which suggested that teachers' conceptions of students and their subsequent behavior toward those students might influence their achievement.

In the *Pygmalion* project (Rosenthal & Jacobson, 1968), teachers were given false information about a randomly chosen subset of students. Investigators reported that their test scores could predict which students were about to bloom intellectually. There was no reason to believe that students identified as bloomers would achieve higher than comparable students for reasons other than the belief that these researchers attempted to create in the mind of the teachers. Part of the controversy that surrounded the original study was because no observational data were collected to see if teachers behaved differently toward students described to them as potential bloomers than they did toward other similar students who were not identified as bloomers. However, process work on how performance expectations were communicated quickly followed (Good, 1969; Brophy & Good, 1970). Further controversy revolved around the fact that false expectations were created by experimenters; however, work quickly emerged to illustrate that teachers themselves were capable of creating expectations on their own (Palardy, 1969; Seaver, 1971). It is important to note that the original Rosenthal and Jacobson study was controversial because of various methodological problems that threatened the veracity of the findings (Elashoff & Snow, 1971).

Pygmalion in the Classroom (Rosenthal & Jacobson, 1968) touched off a flurry of studies that explored the possible role of teacher expectancies in students' learning. These results provided potentially rich policy implications in areas with high enrollment of minority students. For example, Cooper and Good (1983) noted

> The implications of *Pygmalion's* results for minority pupils and children from low SES backgrounds was a special source of concern since these pupils might project cues that would make it easy for teachers to underestimate their potential. (p. xi)

What follows is a brief summary of some of that knowledge that has been garnered over the past 3 decades.

DEBUNKING MISCONCEPTIONS

Differential Behavior Does Not (Always) Equal a Self-Fulfilling Prophecy

Even when teachers exhibit differential behavior toward students on the basis of their "putative" achievement levels (or any other characteristic), these teacher expectations are not automatically self-fulfilling. Students may prevent expectations from becoming fulfilled by resisting them in distinct ways that cause teachers to change their original expectations (Brophy & Good, 1970).

Differential Behavior Can Be Adaptive

It has long been understood that differential teacher behavior is not necessarily inappropriate in classroom settings (Alpert, 1974). Low-achieving students, for example, may initially need more structure than high-achieving students (Snow, Corno, & Jackson, 1996). Accordingly, criteria have been developed for use in assessing when patterns of differential behavior suggest inadequate, inappropriate student treatment (Good & Brophy, 2000). Ferguson (1998a) also provided a conceptual analysis of criteria that define three models of differential treatment. And, for some time it has been recognized that differential interaction patterns can be caused by students as well as teachers (Brophy & Good, 1974; West & Anderson, 1976). Hence, the mere presence of differential teacher behavior does not equal low teacher expectations.

Student Mediation

For some time, it has been known that students are aware of teachers' differential behavior toward high- and low-achieving students and that they make judgments about the fairness and appropriateness of such behavior. For example, Good (1969) wrote

> Students vary greatly in their threshold for decoding information and realizing that a particular statement means "I am a good student." Equally apparent is the phenomenon that students vary with regard to sensitivity and criticism. Some children are thick and impenetrable brick walls, seemingly unaffected by teacher comments; other children are fragile egg shells capable of being cracked by a slight frown from the teacher. (p. 24)

However, over time we have learned much about how students actively mediate teacher expectations. For example, Weinstein and Middlestadt (1979) reported that students were aware that some teachers did not help low achievers with their seatwork and often collect such work before students have a chance to complete it. In some classrooms, students report considerably more differential teacher behavior toward low- and high-achieving students than in other classrooms. It is important to note that in classrooms where students perceived higher levels of differential behavior, teacher expectations had more impact on end-of-year reading scores (Brattesani, Weinstein, & Marshall, 1984).

Not only do students mediate teacher expectations, but they also mediate expectations for each other based on perceived social and academic status. Lloyd and Cohen (1999) found that classrooms vary widely on the degree to which they are congruent. In congruent classrooms, students' perceptions of classmates' social and academic status is highly correlated. Therefore, in congruent settings, only a few students are held to peer-level high expectations, whereas the remaining students are held to moderate or low expectations. Subsequently, when teachers put students into heterogeneous ability groups, students' expectations for one another's performance mediates lower-achieving students' willingness to participate on small group tasks. And, this is especially the case if lower-achieving students are grouped with those students deemed to hold high social and academic status among their peers.

It is interesting to note that in classrooms where status differentiation perceptions vary widely (on social and academic dimensions), students are more likely to monitor their participation, whereas in contrast, when status differentiation is less notable (and expectations for classmates more even), participation by low-achieving students increases. Indeed, the social climate of classrooms and how students' mediate each other's expectations affects students' willingness to participate on structured group tasks.

GROWING AWARENESS OF THE COMPLEXITY OF EXPECTATION EFFECTS

Subject Matter

For many years it has been known that interactions of gender occur in math and reading such that in some classrooms, boys receive better treatment in math classes, whereas girls receive better treatment in reading classes (Leinhardt, Seewald, & Engel, 1979). For example, Palardy (1969) found that in terms of reading achievement, boys achieved less when taught by teachers who did not think that boys could progress as rapidly as girls. In contrast, Jones and Wheatley (1990) examined teacher–student interactions in 30 physical science and 30 chemistry classes. On average, they found that boys received more teacher contact of all types than did girls (positive and negative).

Group and Class Effects

There are data to suggest that teachers interact differentially in ways other than toward individual students. There are, for example, data to show differential behavior toward groups of students (Eder, 1981; Weinstein, 1976) and classes of students (Evertson, 1982; Schrank 1968, 1970). Teachers' behavior toward high and low groups are marked by the provision of unchallenging—and often less interesting—work to low achievers. And, there is a vast literature on tracking to suggest that higher tracks are generally more intellectually stimulating than lower tracks (Ferguson, 1998b; Oakes, 1985). Of course, in some cases differences in the intellectual climate between high track and low track students can be attributed to students; however, in some of this literature, there are designs that amply illustrate teacher effects (Evertson, 1982; Schrank, 1968, 1970).

Teacher Types

All teachers do not differentiate their behavior toward students believed to be more and less capable. In earlier investigations, researchers identified different types of teachers and different explanations as to why teachers did or did not communicate differential expectations to students. For example, Brophy & Good (1974) described proactive teachers, reactive teachers, and overreactive teachers. It was only the overreactive teachers that were seen as behaving in ways that actually further undermined student achievement. Marshall and Weinstein (1984) contended that teachers' beliefs about the nature of intelligence may influence their classroom behavior. That is, some teachers view intelligence as relatively stable and singular in its expression, whereas other teachers see intelligence as incremental and that it can be improved. Hence, it has become clearer over time that teacher's beliefs about the malleability of intelligence interacts with beliefs about individual students. More recently, Babad (1998) argued that teachers' affective reactions as well as their cognitive beliefs partly determine teachers' differential behavior.

Student Types

Students are not equally susceptible to expectations effects. Weinstein and McKown (1998) made the point that although most students are aware of differential teacher behavior, it is likely that only some students are especially vulnerable to teacher expectation effects. Frank (1963) summarized the personality traits of patients who were most responsive to placebo treatments in medical research and noted that other-directed participants were especially likely to show placebo effects. Johnson (1970) suggested that students who are dependent, adult-oriented, and generally other-directed would be especially vulnerable to expectation effects. Persell (1977) and West and Anderson (1976) suggested that younger and more dependent students are more likely to be influenced by teachers.

Salonen, Lehtinen, and Olkinuora (1998) reported that in Finnish classrooms, students and teachers exerted reciprocal influences. Students, using skills learned at home, can influence teachers to give them unneeded help, and so forth. Salonen et al. (1998) noted

> Low achieving children differ from their high-achieving peers not only in regard to cognitive–strategic skills, but also in the ways they are motivationally, emotionally, and socially "tuned" to academic performance situations. (p. 119)

They distinguished three types of student orientation (task-oriented, ego-defensive, and socially dependent) and suggested that these differing orientations lead students to interpret teachers' behavior differentially. Because of the way in which they mediate and respond to teachers, different types of students also influence teachers' behavior during the course of the year.

RESEARCH CONSIDERATIONS

Theoretical Models

Various theoretical models have been developed to explain teachers' differential behavior toward students believed to be more and less capable (Brophy & Good, 1970; Good & Weinstein, 1986; Rosenthal, 1974). And, there is an evolving ongoing debate about different theoretical lenses that might be used to explain teachers' differential behavior toward students believed to be more and less capable, including ways in which student characteristics and behavior influence teacher behavior. New models have expanded expectancy theory in important ways. For example, Cooper (1979) argued persuasively that for some teachers, the differential behavior offered students may be more on the basis of control than ability per se. He contended that teachers perceive the classroom behavior of highs as more controllable and predictable than that of students they perceive to be low achievers. And, in this sense, highs may be called on more by teachers because they present them with fewer problems. In contrast, other models have given more importance to students' attributions and interpretations of classroom events (e.g., Darley & Fazio, 1980; Weinstein & Middlestadt, 1979).[2]

Changing Methodology

Over time, other insights about the way in which teachers' and students' expectations for one another influence classroom behavior have been developed. Much of the early work

[2]Many other models have been proposed. For a discussion of some of these models, see Babad (1998).

on teacher expectations relied on observational measures of teacher and student behaviors in classrooms. Subsequently, researchers made use of students' reports of classroom events, and there are strong data to suggest that students are aware of differential behavior and have different models for interpreting whether teachers' behavior toward students is inappropriate. Further, investigators have explored time-of-year effects, between- and within-classroom effects (Cooper & Good, 1983), and longitudinal designs have been used to assess whether expectancy effects accumulate over time (Jussim et al., 1998).

Intervention Efforts

There have been several studies showing that feedback to teachers can change their behavior toward students perceived as high and low achievers (Good & Brophy, 1974). Mason, Schroeter, Combs, and Washington (1992) found that when eighth-grade students, whose scores did not qualify them for prealgebra classes, were assigned to those courses anyway, the higher course content and teacher expectations were associated with positive student achievement. Students enrolled in prealgebra classes benefited from the higher placement as compared to students with comparable pretest scores who in the previous year were assigned to general math. Subsequently, students who were allowed to take prealgebra enrolled in more advanced mathematics classes in high school and had higher grades in those classes than the comparison group (from the year before) who were denied access to prealgebra. Hence, when the structured expectation of an "acceptable pretest" score was widened, students performed well in the course in which they would have otherwise been denied admission. Others have developed more comprehensive intervention models involving multiple teachers who are working with enhancing expectations and performance (Weinstein et al., 1991).

RESEARCH IN RELATED AND EMERGING AREAS

Differential Expectations in Home and School

There is growing recognition that certain types of "management" and "work" differ between schools and homes, especially low income minority homes. McCaslin and Murdoch (1991) showed how varied definitions of work can be between home and school and how such differences can undercut student academic performance. For example, in a case study comparing two students from working class homes, they noted that the students' homes differed in parental authority and that in both cases, students internalized parental values:

> The cases also illustrate the evolving congruence between home and school expectations: Julio's home learning is becoming less effective as an approach to learning in school. In contrast, as Nora progresses through school, her home learning will likely serve her even better than it did in earlier grades. (p. 253)

Ferguson (1998b) argued that in some instances, the behavioral and work patterns appropriate in lower class Black homes do not match those expectations of "appropriate maturity" in first-grade classes. Specifically, he noted that Black parents often hold ambiguous attitudes toward education and therefore, young students look more heavily to their teachers for what is academically expected. Further, in many Black families, management is focused more on conduct than on task. This may be in part why some Black students prefer an authoritative teacher style (Siddle-Walker, 1992).

It is important to understand that cultural differences across groups make it likely that the correspondence or mismatch between home and school will take different forms. For example, students from Hispanic homes may prefer classrooms that are more cooperative than authoritative (Casanova & Arias, 1993; Moll 1992), and many Hispanic students respond to *Abrazo* (personal support). In many American Indian homes, value is placed on group membership and cohesiveness; hence, initial teacher criticism and praise is more appropriately communicated privately (Maker & Schieber , 1989). Asian American students' families value academic achievement, persistence, and personal responsibility. In contrast, students in these families are less likely to learn assertiveness and risk taking skills (Kitano, 1989; Tanaka, 1989). Although insight into family values that differ across ethnic groups and socioeconomic status is important, teachers must be sure to use such information as a starting point. All students in time need to learn assertiveness and cooperative skills.

Social Motivation

The combined effects of students' academic and social competencies as they relate to the communication of teachers' differential expectations is an emerging area of inquiry. As the importance of learners' social context grows (Turner & Meyer, 2000), it is becoming more popular to consider the combined effects of student academic and social characteristics (i.e., instead of their separate effects). One area where this merger is becoming increasingly evident is the field of student social motivation where researchers analyze the combined effects of peer and teacher relationships and individual motivational variables on subsequent academic performance (Juvonen & Wentzel, 1996).

The evolving nature of students' social relationships with teachers and peers is related to grade-level changes in motivational orientation. In general, as students progress from the elementary grades to the middle school grades, they tend to shift from being predominantly intrinsically motivated to being more extrinsically motivated—an outcome typically explained by the shift from more personal attention in elementary school to an increased emphasis on competition, social comparison, and grades in the middle school years (Eccles & Midgley, 1988). Harter (1996) hypothesized that individual differences in perceived scholastic competence mediated these grade-level shifts in academic emphasis (i.e., students with higher perceived scholastic competence tended to hold more stable intrinsic motivational tendencies, whereas students with lower perceived scholastic competence tended to fluctuate more with the transition from elementary to middle school classrooms). A student's social environment plays a role in healthy academic and social outcomes. As it becomes increasingly important to acknowledge the saliency of students' social culture, it will become more important to investigate the nature of the complex association between students' social relationships and their academic outcomes (Lee & Smith, 1999).

One way to consider student variables such as motivation and social competence in classroom contexts is to investigate the reciprocal relation between social competency and teacher expectations. Students come to the classroom with different levels of prosocial behavior. Some students know how to meld to the rules of the classroom more easily than do other students. Because these students are more "controllable," it is likely that many teachers will find their cooperation rewarding. Further, as we note later, there is evidence in the early grades that teachers allow maturity level and student management behavior to lower academic grades.

TOWARD AN EARLY INTERVENTION OF MINORITY FIRST GRADERS

Hence, conceptions of expectations have evolved to include many new aspects, including the distinction between social and academic performance, motivational variables, and the importance of context. Historically, the field has been rather general in its location of expectation effects. As the work by Mason et al. (1992) and Weinstein et al. (1991) illustrated, the power of intervention may be to bring general knowledge of expectations to bear on a particular context.

We now turn to a future-oriented application of needed expectancy research for improving in a particular setting the performance of Black students from low income homes in first-grade classrooms. As we discuss in the following section, data suggest that Black and White students are not equally susceptible to teachers' differential behavior in the classroom. Some have argued that differences in students' vulnerability to teacher expectations, in part, helps to explain the achievement gap commonly found between Black and White students (Ferguson, 1998a). In the following section, we review the literature on expectation effects as they occur in first-grade classrooms for both Black and White children. Subsequently, we argue for more systematic research and an intervention plan that addresses this achievement gap.[3]

Teachers' Interactions With Black Students

Casteel (1997) asked eighth- and ninth-grade students about who they most wanted to please with their classwork. Interestingly, there were notable differences based on gender and ethnicity. The answer was "teachers" for 81% of Black girls, 62% of Black boys, 28% of White girls, and 32% of White boys. In contrast, White students were more concerned with pleasing parents than were Black students.

Ferguson (1998a) wondered if, on average, Black students may give teachers less positive reinforcement than White students with similar abilities. It has been known for some time that teachers' feelings about students as social beings as well as academic learners impact how teachers interact differentially with students. Ferguson (1998a) extrapolated from the research from Willis and Brophy (1974) to suggest that, on average, teachers likely prefer to teach Whites and, on average, they probably provide White students more plentiful and unambiguous support than Black students. However, Ferguson (1998a) noted that race of teacher is not necessarily a critical variable:

> Mismatches of race between teachers and students do not appear to be the central problem. Even Black teachers need help in learning to cope with some of the special demands that Black children from disadvantaged backgrounds may present. (p. 299)

Although Casteel (1997) reported that Black eighth and ninth graders were more willing to please their teachers, whereas their White peers were more concerned about satisfying parents, these differences may be more a comment on parenting than about teachers. He wondered if it is possible that White parents more consistently pressure their children for good grades, whereas Black parents are less assertive about grades and depend on teacher judgements and reports.[4] Our guess is that the issue is more likely to be income, time, and information differences among parents, not race per se. For example, some research suggests that divorced mothers, as a group, have lowered expectations for their children's academic work and may be satisfied with lower school grades (Barber, 1995; Barber & Eccles, 1991). Parents who are coping with various issues may have little time to mediate low teacher expectations for their children.

[3] We believe that intervention in first grade is important for all students who come from low income homes. Here we address but one important context—Black students from low income homes.

[4] It is important to note that parents in this research and in Casteel's (1997) work were primarily White.

Jones (1989) found that Black students were more likely to be seen as less capable than White students and that teachers underestimated the ability of Black students relative to their actual achievement. Further, this effect was more common in high differentiation classes (i.e., classes in which students reported that teachers exhibited more differential behavior).[5] Ironically, the pressure on students from low income homes to please their teachers may be sufficiently intense to "undermine" quality of teacher contact. For example, some students have to deal with issues such as, "Will the teacher think I wasn't listening or that I'm not smart if I ask this question?" Or, they may overgeneralize teacher feedback cues. For example, a student talking to the teacher privately may overreact to the teacher's nonverbal look of concern that is directed not to the student but that was stimulated by other students in the classroom who are misbehaving. Not enough recognition has been paid to the possibility of teachers' expectations being influenced not just by "ability" cues (the clarity of the students' questions), but also social cues (students' ability to know when to ask a question, students' ability to express empathy toward other students, etc.).

Ferguson (1998a) presented a re-analysis of data based on research conducted by Jussim, Eccles, and Madon (1996). In Jussim et al.'s (1996) original study, data indicated that teacher expectation effects were stronger with African American students than with White students, as indicated by teachers' performance ratings of students in October and students' grades and performance on the Michigan Educational Assessment Program (MEAP) test in May. Ferguson's (1998a) re-analysis separated students by ethnicity (Black or White) and original teacher performance ratings from October (students were grouped based on five performance ratings) to show how strongly expectation effects interacted with ethnicity as measured by students' predicted May grades and scores on the MEAP. Black students who received the highest performance rating in October were predicted by teachers to outperform White students who received the same rating by .43 standard deviation units (SDU) based on their grades and by .31 SDU based on their MEAP scores. In contrast, Black students who received the lowest rating in October were predicted to underperform White students with the same rating by .51 SDU on their MEAP scores, and by .57 SDU on their grades. Ferguson (1998a) reported

> This would represent stereotype bias for expected progress, even if there is no such bias in the evaluation of October performance. The accuracy of the stereotype might reflect self-fulfilling prophecy in the teachers' expectation, or it might not. Evidence that teacher perceptions affect subsequent performance more for Blacks than for Whites suggests either that Black students respond differently than Whites to similar treatment from teachers, or that teachers treat Black and White students differently, or both. (pp. 288–289)

Ferguson (1998a, 1998b) argued persuasively that Black students, especially in early grades, often receive less stimulating and supportive environments than do White students. Interestingly, he reviewed work on class size to suggest that Black students, especially in inner city schools, are more likely to gain from smaller classes than are White students. We suspect that this is the case in some classes because the smaller class size allows the teacher to be less rushed and hence, can spend more time with lower-achieving students. With more time, students respond more and teachers have more time to clarify or to more fully understand a student's thinking. Furthermore, the more relaxed setting may help the student to attend more fully to academic exchange per se and to place less emphasis on performance per se—pleasing the teacher. There is evidence to suggest that memory of specific events can be disturbed if individuals are too intent on suppressing emotion (e.g., disappointment in failing the teacher; Richards & Gross, 2000); hence, the smaller class size can allow students to be more active listeners and to pay more attention to the cognitive aspects of the exchange (more on this is presented later). Given the interest that Black students have in pleasing the teacher, a smaller, more individualized classroom may be critical if achievement is to be enhanced.

First Grade—A Critical Point

The power of first-grade settings has been demonstrated in several studies. Good (1969) found that first-grade teachers afforded students who were believed to be more capable more response opportunities. Brophy and Good (1970) found that first-grade students believed to be less capable received from teachers fewer response opportunities, were more likely to be criticized when they gave an incorrect answer, were less likely to be praised when they gave a correct answer, and were more likely to be given up on (the teacher calls on someone else) when they failed to respond or responded incorrectly to a teacher question. Hence, students believed to be less capable had fewer response opportunities and a less supportive environment. These interactions would cause at least some of these students to focus more on avoiding response opportunities rather than focusing on the task itself.

Weinstein (1976) did not find differences in how first-grade teachers treated high and low reading groups, but she did find that group placement had predictable effects on students. After controlling for differences in readiness scores, placement in the high group facilitated student achievement whereas placement in the low group lowered achievement. Donna Eder's (1981) work illustrated that children with overlapping reading abilities were placed into higher or lower reading groups in first grade primarily on the basis of their ma-

[5]Again, we do not feel that race is necessarily the dominant factor. The key issue is probably low income environments in which parents have fewer resources (especially time) and may interact in more direct ways with their children than do parents from higher socioeconomic backgrounds.

turity level. Hence, this practice made the lower reading group a less supportive learning environment because proportionately it included more students with shorter attention spans and less impulse control. Eder (1981), unlike Weinstein (1976), also demonstrated a teacher effect and noted that teachers spent considerably less time on instructional activities in the lower than the higher reading group and that these differences in instruction largely accounted for differential student performance that emerged. Hence, over time, students in the lower group became less competent readers than students of similar abilities who were placed into the higher group because, in part, the instructional environment was less meaningful and supportive than that afforded the higher group.

It is well established that under certain conditions, teachers' differential beliefs and behavior can be related to student performance. For example, how well students do in their initial school experiences are sharp predictors of their subsequent performance. Entwisle, Alexander, and Olson (1997) put it this way:

> [T]he child's first marks in first grade strongly forecasts marks throughout elementary school and in some way they are even more reliable bell weathers of first performance than test scores because they are sensitive to the child's gender, ethnicity, and economic background. (p. 12)

Empirical support for this contention can be found in Entwisle and Alexander (1988), who reported that Black students received lower marks in first grade than White students even though their test scores on entering school were as high. Similarly, Hess et al. (1969) reported that boys (but not girls) were graded lower than their actual achievement scores suggested and that first- and second-grade students' academic marks were influential in part because of conduct grades. Black students—especially boys—and to a lesser extent other children who come from low income homes, may find their academic scores improperly lowered because of classroom conduct.

What students learn in first grade. Good (1981) suggested that teachers may induce passivity in some lower-achieving students. This is especially likely in kindergarten through second-grade classes. First, considering that low-achieving students are less likely to be able to answer correctly in the first place and that their mistakes occur in public, low achievers must face considerably more than the usual degrees of ambiguity and risk that are built into classroom interactions (Jackson, 1968). Given the ambiguity of public response, a strategy for them may be to remain passive—not to volunteer and not to respond when called on, and, as shown in some classes, teachers reinforce this student action by quickly giving up on these students.

A second factor that might lead to their passivity is that low-achieving students, in comparison to other students, must adjust to more varied teacher expectations. Their teachers might treat them inconsistently over the course of the school year, trying one approach after another in an attempt to find something that works. Further, they may have more than one teacher at a given time (if they are involved in remedial or special education) who differ in their strategies for trying to work with low achievers. As Good (1981) argued, some teachers minimize interactions with low achievers and treat them coolly when they do interact. However, others seek them out frequently and provide a good deal of encouragement and support. Some teachers call on them frequently in an attempt to get them to participate more often, but others mostly avoid them. Some rarely praise their successes, but others praise almost everything they do, even responses that are not correct. Student passivity is a likely outcome of such diversity of treatment and expectations. Not knowing what to do, low achievers may learn to avoid initiations and wait for the teacher to structure their behavior.

Good, Slavings, Harel, and Emerson (1987) found that students in first-grade classrooms who were seen as less capable by teachers were willing to ask teachers as many academic questions as those students who were seen as more capable. However, in third-grade classrooms in the same schools, more lowly rated students were found to ask fewer questions to teachers than peers who were rated higher by their teachers. This research was cross-sectional (i.e., not longitudinal), but it provides indirect evidence that some students learn "their place" in the social status of the classroom and become less active learners. Perhaps in socializing students to the norms of the classroom, teachers inadvertently contribute to lowered student initiative (e.g., students think their questions are being criticized when in actuality, the teacher is simply trying to communicate that it's the wrong time for a question).

In students' immediate responses to teachers, it is easy to suspect that on occasion, the students who desperately want to please the teacher may be so embarrassed when they cannot answer a question that they do not hear the teacher's (or another student's) subsequent explanation. There is growing evidence to suggest that certain types of emotional regulation impairs cognitive functioning. Richards and Gross (2000) reported that in laboratory and field research, participants' attempts to suppress emotion (e.g., control a facial expression) lowered performance on an objective memory task. If children interpret their inability to answer a teacher's comment as a threat to their self-worth (evoking high anxiety or distress), then students may be more focused on hiding their disappointment than on learning from the corrective feedback. Further, the nonverbal frustration on the face of the student may even prevent the teacher from providing needed corrective information to the student. Unfortunately, however, some students do not get corrective feedback (Brophy & Good, 1970), even though the power of corrective feedback has been demonstrated (Guskey, 1982).

Many American policymakers are concerned about grade inflation and social promotion. Around the country, schools are retaining more students, requiring summer school, or both. However, it has been known for some time that grading practices can be too low as well as too high. Entwisle and Hayduk (1978) compared grades that were given in schools serving middle income and low income populations. The average grade in the working class school was almost a full grade below that in the middle class school. Students in the low income school primarily received Cs and Ds, whereas students in the middle income school mainly received As and Bs. It seems a ludicrous way to introduce students to school by giving them grades that stress to students that they are marginal or inadequate students.

What parents learn in first-grade classes. Many would contend that the biggest influences on first graders' (and kindergartners') beliefs about their academic capabilities and performance stem mainly from parents and teachers. In comparison to older students, most first graders are motivated simply by the desire to please adults—namely teachers and parents. Parents, especially those from low income homes, are also vulnerable to teacher beliefs about their children's academic performance. This is especially the case when parents are new to the educational system (i.e., their children were not previously enrolled in preschool settings that stressed academics) because they have less experience with structured, "appropriate" academic interactions with their children. Indeed, kindergartners and first-grade students (and their parents) are being informed of their relative ability from teachers whose expectations of performance stem from student comparisons within each class well as comparisons teachers make of students from year to year.

If, in fact, teachers' beliefs overlap with those of the child's parent (or guardian), it is likely that the beliefs (e.g., the grade assigned by the teacher) are an accurate description of a child's reading ability and therefore, the two adult minds may influence the young child's thinking in marked ways. The contention is that if teachers and parents see the child as a capable learner, the opportunities afforded such student would be strikingly different than if both saw the child as of marginal ability. And, to reiterate, some—perhaps many—low income parents are going to base their performance expectations for their own child on feedback from the teacher.

Can parents mediate teachers' low expectations for their child? It would seem reasonable to argue that they could under certain circumstances, but first, only if they believe that their son or daughter is more capable than the level described by the teacher, and then only if they have the resources and skills to do so. Some parents are sufficiently overwhelmed by life circumstances that they have little time or inclination to seek out teachers. Other parents have the volition and skills needed to seek out teachers, share information, and develop cooperative strategies for improving a student's ability to read. Hence, parents need both a belief in their child's ability to read, as well as skills in communicating with the teacher.

In contrast, some parents have only medium levels of beliefs about their child's potential performance level (e.g., "she's just another kid") or hold no expectations for performance; hence, when they find that their son or daughter is placed in the second or third reading group, they are not concerned. Ironically, when the first report card comes home with a low grade from the teacher in reading, this communication may serve to lower and solidify the parents' expectation for performance. That is, the teacher placed the child in an "easier" group[6] and still the child does poorly—what would have happened if the child had been placed in the more demanding curriculum? Parents do not understand that in many cases, the assignment of a student into the second or third reading group guarantees that the child will receive a lower grade—no matter how well they do—than any child placed in the high group.

Addressing the Achievement Gap: An Intervention Strategy

Earlier we mentioned two of the many intervention studies that have focused on improving teachers' expectations for low achieving students (Mason et al., 1992; Weinstein et al., 1991). Although these studies only examined achievement with older students, there is reason to believe that intervention in the first grade (or earlier) might be an important intervention context. In the following sections, we propose a general approach for intervention strategies designed to enhance the achievement of low income students in their first year of formal schooling. We believe that our intervention, grounded in expectancy theory, is important from a social policy perspective as its attempts to decrease initial and long-term racial differences in students' achievement test scores (Jencks & Phillips, 1998).

Teachers. Unfortunately, there is growing evidence to suggest that the quality of instruction in many schools serving low income students is not as high as in schools serving students from high income homes (Ferguson, 1998b). Therefore, we argue that a solid intervention strategy begins with high-quality instruction and well-prepared teachers. As part of their preparation, all teachers should be provided with a solid background in expectancy theory so that they realize that expectancies can be too high or too low and become aware of the many ways that teachers can provide positive or negative feedback (see Good & Brophy, 2000, for content details; see Weinstein et al., 1991, for process suggestions). Further, teachers need information about effective approaches to reading instruction (see Mayer, 2001).

[6]The work by Eder (1981) illustrates that placement into a lower ability reading group actually makes it harder for students to learn.

Every effort should be made to keep class size small in first-grade classrooms. There is evidence to suggest that low income students generally, and Black low income students specifically, are apt to benefit from increased teacher attention that is allowed by smaller classes. Ferguson (1998a) argued that teachers' expectations are too inflexible for Black low income students. A smaller class provides the teachers with opportunities to take longer in interacting with individual students. Such sustained contact with students may help teachers to see more potential in all students.

Teachers need to realize that students who are viewed as less capable may be victims of too much or too little teacher concern and vigilance. Some time ago, Brophy and Good (1970) found that students who were believed to be less capable students by their teachers received treatment by their teachers that would sustain if not widen the gap between these and other students. The pattern of behavior that Brophy and Good (1970) documented (calling less on students believed to be less capable, criticizing students more frequently for wrong answers, etc.) suggests that teachers were not acting appropriately.

Such seemingly illogical behavior may occur in part because classrooms are complex and teachers cannot be aware of all aspects—even some of their own actions. Good & Brophy (1974) found that teachers were generally more aware of the frequency of their behavior than its qualitative aspects. For example, teachers knew that they called on some students less than others in large measure because they did not want to embarrass these students. However, teachers were largely unaware of the qualitative aspects of their behavior (When a student gives a wrong answer, do they stay with the student or call on someone else?). Hence, some of the teachers' responses may be more affective than cognitive and, if cognitive, more focused on an immediate event rather than on a broader institutional strategy.

Ironically, at times teachers' feelings of concern for students may get in the way of good instruction. (e.g., "I don't call on some students to answer challenging questions because I don't want to embarrass them. I really want them to be successful; therefore, I don't praise their answers unless I know that they really know the material."). Hence, displays of "concern" are often a result of inappropriate expectations that are either too low or too high.

Other teachers may reject less capable students (not necessarily categorically) because of short-term frustration or irritation (a student's response is criticized because the teacher is irritated that the student raised a hand when not knowing an answer or because they don't think the student was listening or trying). Such rejection is unlikely to be understood by first graders who may confuse behavioral criticisms with attacks on their global academic potential.

Elsewhere, Ferguson (1998a) argued that teachers' expectations may be too inflexible toward low-achieving students (specifically, he argued toward low-achieving, Black students). We think this is a plausible hypothesis but would add one dimension to this argument. It may be that teachers' unchanging beliefs are maintained by an inconsistent and inappropriate pedagogical approach to these pupils. Either because of excessive concerns of support or rejection, teachers work with these students in fewer situations in which there is calm deliberation and discussion of academic issues. Hence, these students not only fail to obtain (or to attend to) teachers' corrective feedback, but they are also likely to feel that they are not listened to by their teachers.

Teachers need to understand that students' maturity and general conduct must be kept separate from academic performance. Students need to learn appropriate forms of conduct, however, students' general behavior should not be allowed to affect academic assessments. In socializing students to first-grade classrooms, teachers need to be careful that the communication system they use does not confuse social conduct and academic activity. These students need corrective feedback when their classroom behavior is inappropriate, but it is critical that teachers deliver such information without lowering such students' beliefs about their value and potential as learners.

"Seeing is believing" is an important condition for change. We know that many Americans have not strongly rejected the possibility that school achievement is related to genetics and that Black students do poorly in school because they have less academic intelligence (Ferguson, 1998a, 1998b). And, even teachers who believe in the power of the environment and good teaching may find themselves engaging in inappropriate and unproductive teaching strategies.

A number of years ago, Thomas L. Good spoke to the first graduating class of the Teacher Expectations and Student Achievement (TESA) program in Los Angeles, and was impressed by the number of teachers who informally reported that the program was useful because of the rich information contained about expectation communication. However, it is important to note that teachers stressed that what was most important was to see other teachers teaching "low-achieving" students. They reported that such observations helped them to renew their commitment to obtaining higher-quality responses from their students. Hence, any intervention program should include many videotapes of successful performance in many classrooms as well as the chance for teachers to visit and be visited by other teachers.

Further, teachers and schools should reconsider the role of grades in first-grade classrooms. Given the current era of getting tough on students (terminate social promotion, mandatory summer school), teachers may be overly demanding in first-grade classrooms. Teachers should be emphasizing what students do right and what they know, as well as providing corrective feedback.

Students. Students might benefit from attending first-grade classes in the spring before they enroll in the fall. This would allow them to see first-grade behaviors (how to line up, how to work quietly at a desk when the teacher is with other students, etc.). Further, students should be encouraged to attend summer school both before the first grade begins and in the summer that follows. In the initial summer school, students should be exposed to activities that are both stimulating and enjoyable. Importantly, before they enter first grade, they should begin to learn how to evaluate their own academic work (Zuckerman, 1994). Students' capacity for self regulation should be addressed (see Paris & Paris, 2001).

Parents. Parents should receive training about the communication of low expectations as early as the spring before their child enters first grade. They should visit first-grade classrooms and know who will teach their child. Abundant reading materials should be made available to all parents. Parents should realize that first-grade teachers have multiple roles to fulfill and that especially they must socialize students to ways of responding in group settings, as well as helping them to become better learners. Parents should be encouraged to ask teachers about academic performance and conduct and they should have regular meetings with the teacher and stay abreast of work that is assigned in school. On occasion parents should be encouraged to sit in on classes with their child so that they can be knowledgeable about school tasks such as building vocabulary and reading for pleasure. Students have to deal with more than conflicting teacher expectations (e.g., don't make mistakes; don't ask me to help vs. trying to do it before you ask me, etc.), such as conflicting home–school expectations. For example, McCaslin and Murdoch (1991) presented case studies reflecting home and school variations and the importance of "effort." Parents and teachers should be encouraged to explore their mutual conceptions of management, rewards, and conceptions of appropriate social behavior.

Schools and communities. Because of space limitations, we can only touch briefly on two other areas that are critical parts of an expectation intervention: school- and community-level support. Schools vary widely in terms of safety, physical attractiveness, and whether teachers are encouraged to communicate across levels in ways that enhance students' social and academic success. Too many school environments in which inner city students attend are cold, unattractive, and physically intimidating. Efforts must be made to make schools warm environments in which students are welcomed by teachers and older peers. Schools that are in poor shape physically must work even harder to counteract the feelings that inadequate buildings communicate to many students (i.e., society doesn't care about you and your learning).

It is increasingly the case that more adults are out of the home when children return from school. This is of course true across all social classes, but it is especially the case for children who live in poverty. Any program designed to improve the academic performance of kindergarten and first-grade students must find ways to provide students with afternoon care that continues to provide opportunities for both academic and social growth. Students' parents, teachers, schools, and communities need to provide clear expectations for academic success and resources, and experiences that fulfill these expectations.

CONCLUSION

In this article we outlined the findings from over three decades of research on teacher expectations. The field has moved from an initial emphasis on teacher behavior to include more attention to the effects of student mediation, curricular variables, and congruency of teacher expectations across time. Further, we summarized evidence to show that Black students who enter first-grade classrooms in inner city schools are often at a disadvantage compared to students who enter first grade in more affluent neighborhoods. These different opportunity structures are systemic and are embedded in parents, teachers, students themselves, schools, and communities.

Given the provision of inadequate resources afforded some students (no books, dangerous and physically inadequate buildings), some students are exposed to a clear societal expectation: "We care less about you and your education than we do about other students." Some students who enter substandard schools are undoubtedly unaware of their fate, but some are and these students need counter messages that say they are important. At the very least, we argue that students who attend schools serving students from low income schools should enter first-grade classrooms that are small and staffed by high-quality teachers.

We think this literature has a wide base for application, and first-grade intervention is but one strategic point. Among other possible application points, we would argue that many summer school programs and retention plans fail in part because of their inadequate introduction of the role of students', teachers', and parents' expectations about the meaning of the educational opportunity. Further, previous work illustrates that expectancy interventions can have effects at older grade levels (Mason et al., 1992; Weinstein et al., 1991). The potential impact of research on social communication of expectancy effects has relevance for various social policy issues.

REFERENCES

Alpert, J. (1974). Teacher behavior across ability groups: A consideration of the mediation of Pygmalion effects. *Journal of Educational Psychology, 66*, 348–353.

Babad, E. (1998). Preferential affect: The crux of the teacher expectancy issue. In J. Brophy (Ed.), *Advances in research on teaching: Expectations in the classroom* (Vol. 7, pp. 183–214). Greenwich, CT: JAI.

Barber, B. (1995). Preventive intervention with adolescents and divorced mothers: A conceptual framework for program design and evaluation. *Journal of Applied Developmental Psychology, 16*, 481–503.

Barber, B., & Eccles, J. (1991, April). *Divorce and remarriage effects on mothers' performance: Maternal expectations mediate decline*. Paper presented at the biennial meeting of the Society for Research and Child Development.

Berlin, I. (1953). *The hedgehog and the fox: An essay on Tolstoy's view of history*. New York: Simon & Schuster.

Brattesani, K., Weinstein, R., & Marshall, H. (1984). Student perceptions of differential teacher treatment as moderator of teacher expectation effects. *Journal of Educational Psychology, 76*, 236–247.

Brophy, J. (1998). Introduction. In J. Brophy (Ed.), *Advances in research on teaching: Expectations in the classroom* (Vol. 7, pp. ix–xvii). Greenwich, CT: JAI.

Brophy, J., & Good, T. (1970). Teacher's communication of differential expectations for children's classroom performance: Some behavioral data. *Journal of Educational Psychology, 61*, 365–374.

Brophy, J., & Good, T. (1974). *Teacher–student relationships: Causes and consequences*. New York: Holt, Rinehart & Winston.

Casanova, U., & Arias, M. (1993). Contextualizing bilingual education. In M. Arias & U. Casanova (Eds.), *Bilingual education: Politics, practice, and research* (Part II, pp. 1–35). Chicago: University of Chicago Press.

Casteel, C. (1997, April). Attitudes of African-American and Caucasian eighth grade students about praises, rewards, and punishments. *Elementary School Guidance and Counseling, 31*, 262–272.

Clark, K. (1963). Educational stimulation of racially disadvantaged children. In A. H. Passow (Ed.), *Education in depressed areas* (pp. 142–162). New York: Teachers College Press.

Cooper, H. (1979). Pygmalion grows up: A model for teacher expectation communication and performance influence. *Review of Educational Research, 49*, 389–410.

Cooper, H., & Good, T. (1983). *Pygmalion grows up: Studies in the expectation communication process*. New York: Longman.

Darley, J., & Fazio, R. (1980). Expectancy confirmation processes arising in the social interaction sequence. *American Psychologist, 35*, 867–881.

Davis, A., & Dollard, J. (1940). *Children of bondage*. Washington, DC: American Council on Education.

Ebbinghaus, H. (1913). *Memory*. New York: Teachers College, Press. (Original work published 1885)

Eccles, J., & Midgley, C. (1988). Stage-environment fit: Developmentally appropriate classrooms for young adolescents. In R. E. Ames & C. Ames (Eds.), *Research on motivation in education, goals and cognitions* (Vol. 3, pp. 139–186). New York: Academic.

Eder, D. (1981). Ability grouping as a self-fulfilling prophecy: A micro-analysis of teacher–student interaction. *Sociology of Education, 54*, 151–161.

Elashoff, J., & Snow, R. (1971). *Pygmalion reconsidered*. Belmont, CA: Wadsworth.

Entwisle, D., & Alexander, K. (1988). Factors affecting achievement test scores and marks received by Black and White first graders. *Elementary School Journal, 88*, 449–471.

Entwisle, D., Alexander, K., & Olson, L. (1997). *Children, schools, and inequality*. Boulder, CO: Westview.

Entwisle, D., & Hayduk, A. (1978). Too great expectations. Baltimore: Johns Hopkins University Press.

Evertson, C. (1982). Differences in instructional activities in higher- and lower-achieving junior high English and math classes. *Elementary School Journal, 82*, 329–350.

Ferguson, R. (1998a). Teachers' perceptions and expectations and the Black–White test score gap. In C. Jencks & M. Phillips (Eds.), *The Black–White test score gap* (pp. 273–317). Washington, DC: Brookings Institute.

Ferguson, R. (1998b). Can schools narrow the Black–White test score gap? In C. Jencks & M. Phillips (Eds.), *The Black–White test score gap* (pp. 318–374). Washington, DC: Brookings Institute.

Frank, J. (1963). *Persuasion and healing*. New York: Shocken Books.

Good, T. (1969). *Differential opportunities for student response opportunity and achievement*. Unpublished doctoral dissertation, Indiana University, Bloomington.

Good, T. (1970). Which pupils do teachers call on? *Elementary School Journal, 70*, 190–198.

Good, T. (1981). Teacher expectations and student perceptions: A decade of research. *Educational Leadership, 38*, 415–423.

Good, T., & Brophy, J. (1974). Changing teacher and student behavior: An empirical investigation. *Journal of Educational Psychology, 66*, 390–405.

Good, T., & Brophy, J. (2000). *Looking in classrooms* (8th ed.). New York: Longman.

Good, T., Sikes, J., & Brophy, J. (1973). Effects of teacher sex and student sex on classroom interaction. *Journal of Educational Psychology, 65*, 74–87.

Good, T., Slavings, R., Harel, K., & Emerson, H. (1987). Student passivity. A study of student question asking in K–12 classrooms. *Sociology of Education, 60*, 181–190.

Good, T., & Thompson, E. K. (1998). Research on the communication of performance expectations: A review of recent perspectives. In J. Brophy (Ed.), *Advances in research on teaching: Expectations in the classroom* (Vol. 7, pp. 273–308). Greenwich, CT: JAI.

Good, T., & Weinstein, R. (1986). Teacher expectations: A framework for exploring classrooms. In K. Zumwalt (Ed.), *Improving teaching (the 1986 ASCD Yearbook)*. Alexandria, VA: Association for Supervision and Curriculum Development.

Guskey, T. (1982). The effects of change in instructional effectiveness on the relationship of teacher expectations and student achievement. *Journal of Educational Research, 75*, 345–348.

Harter, S. (1996). Teacher and classmate influences on scholastic motivation, self-esteem, and level of voice in adolescents. In J. Juvonen & K. Wentzel (Eds.), *Social motivation: Understanding children's school adjustment*. New York: Cambridge University Press.

Heath, S. (1983). *Ways with words*. New York: Cambridge University Press.

Hess, R., Shipman, V., Brophy, J., & Bear, R. (in collaboration with A. Adelberger). (1969). *The cognitive environments of urban preschool children: Follow-up phase*. University of Chicago (mimeo, final report).

Hoehn, A. (1954). A study of social status differentiation in the classroom behavior of 19 third-grade teachers. *Journal of Social Psychology, 39*, 269–262.

Jackson, P. (1968). *Life in classrooms*. New York: Holt, Rinehart & Winston.

Jencks, C. (1972). The Coleman Report and the conventional wisdom. In F. Mosteller & D. Moynihan (Eds.), *On equality of educational opportunity* (pp. 69–115). New York: Random House.

Jencks, C. (1978). Foreword. In B. Heyns (Ed.), *Summer learning and the effects of schooling* (pp. xi–xvi). New York: Academic.

Jencks, C., & Phillips, M. (1998). (Eds.). *The Black–White test score gap*. Washington, DC: Brookings Institute.

Johnson, D. (1970). *The social psychology of education*. New York: Holt, Rinehart & Winston.

Jones, L. (1989). *Teacher expectations for Black and White students in contrasting classroom environments*. Unpublished master's thesis, University of California, Berkeley.

Jones, M., & Wheatley, J. (1990). Gender differences in student–teacher interactions. *Journal of Research in Science Teaching, 27*, 861–874.

Jussim, L., Eccles, J., & Madon, S. (1996). Social perception, social stereotypes, and teacher expectations: Accuracy and the quest for the powerful self-fulfilling prophecy. *Advances in Experimental Social Psychology, 28*, 281–387.

Jussim, L., Smith, A., Madon, S., & Palumbo, P. (1998). Teacher expectations. In J. Brophy (Ed.), *Advances in research on teaching: Expectations in the classroom* (Vol. 7, pp. 1–48). Greenwich, CT: JAI.

Juvonen, J., & Wentzel, K. (1996). (Eds.). *Social motivation: Understanding children's school adjustment*. New York: Cambridge University Press.

Katz, L. (1972). Developmental stages of preschool teachers. *Elementary School Journal, 73,* 50–54.

Kitano, M. (1989). Critique of identification of gifted Asian–American students. In C. Maker & S. Schieber (Eds.), *Defensible programs for cultural and ethnic minorities* (Vol. II, pp. 163–168). Austin, TX: Pro-Ed.

Leacock, E. (1969). *Teaching and learning in city schools.* New York: Basic Books.

Lee, V., & Smith, J. (1999). Social support and achievement: For young adolescents in Chicago: The role of school academic press. *American Educational Research Journal, 36,* 907–945.

Leinhardt, G., Seewald, A., & Engel, M. (1979). Learning what's taught: Sex differences in instruction. *Journal of Educational Psychology, 71,* 432–439.

Lippitt, R., & Gold, M. (1959). Classroom social structure as a mental health problem. *Journal of Social Issues, 15,* 40–49.

Lloyd, P., & Cohen, E. (1999). Peer status in the middle schools: A natural treatment for unequal participation. *Social Psychology of Education, 3,* 193–216.

Maker, C., & Schieber, S. (1989). (Eds.). *Defensible programs for cultural and ethnic minorities* (Vol. II). Austin, TX: Pro-Ed.

Marshall, H., & Weinstein, R. (1984, April). *Classrooms where students perceive high and low amounts of differential teacher treatment.* Paper presented at the annual meeting of the American Educational Research Association, New Orleans, LA.

Mason, D., Schroeter, D., Combs, R., & Washington, K. (1992). Assigning average achieving eighth graders to advanced mathematics classes in an urban junior high. *Elementary School Journal, 92,* 587–599.

Mayer, R. E. (2001). What good is educational psychology? The case of cognition and instruction. *Educational Psychologist, 36,* 83–88.

McCaslin, M., & Good, T. (1996). The informal curriculum. In D. Berliner & R. Calfee (Eds.), *Handbook of educational psychology* (pp. 622–673). New York: Macmillan.

McCaslin, M., & Murdoch, T. (1991). The emergent interaction of home and school in the development of students' adaptive learning. In M. Maehr & P. Pintrich (Eds.), *Advances in motivation and achievement* (Vol. 7, pp. 213–260). Greenwich, CT: JAI.

Merton, R. K. (1948). The self-fulfilling prophecy. *Antioch Review, 8,* 193–210.

Meyer, W., & Thompson, G. (1956). Sex differences and the distribution of teacher approval and disapproval among sixth-grade children. *Journal of Educational Psychology, 47,* 385–396.

Moll, L. (1992). Bilingual classroom studies and community analysis. *Educational Researcher, 21,* 20–24.

Oakes, J. (1985). *Keeping track: How schools structure inequality.* New Haven, CT: Yale University Press.

Palardy, J. (1969). What teachers believe—What children achieve. *Elementary School Journal, 69,* 370–374.

Paris, S. G., & Paris, A. H. (2001). Classroom applications of research on self-regulated learning. *Educational Psychologist, 36,* 89–101.

Persell, C. (1977). *Education and inequality: The roots and results of stratification in American schools.* New York: Free Press.

Rice, S. A. (1929). Contagious bias in the interview: A methodological note. *American Journal of Sociology, 35,* 420–423.

Richards, J. M., & Gross, J. J. (2000). Emotion regulation and memory: The cognitive costs of keeping one's cool. *Journal of Personality and Social Psychology, 79,* 410–424.

Rosenthal, R. (1974). *On the social psychology of the self-fulfilling prophecy: Further evidence for Pygmalion effects and their mediating mechanisms.* New York: MSS Modular Publications.

Rosenthal, R. (1985). From unconscious experimenter bias to teacher expectancy effects. In J. Dusek, V. Hall, & W. Meyer (Eds.), *Teacher expectancies.* Hillsdale, NJ: Lawrence Erlbaum Associates, Inc.

Rosenthal, R., & Jacobson, L. (1968). *Pygmalion in the classroom: Teacher expectation and pupils' intellectual development.* New York: Holt.

Salonen, P., Lehtinen, E., & Olkinuora, E. (1998). Expectations and beyond: The development of motivation and learning in a classroom context. In J. Brophy (Ed.), *Advances in research on teaching: Expectations in the classroom* (Vol. 7, pp. 111–150). Greenwich, CT: JAI.

Schrank, W. (1968). The labeling effect of ability grouping. *Journal of Educational Research, 62,* 51–52.

Schrank, W. (1970). A further study of the labeling effects of ability grouping. *Journal of Educational Research, 63,* 358–380.

Seaver, W. (1971). *Effects of naturally induced teacher expectancies on the academic performance of pupils in primary grades.* Unpublished doctoral dissertation, University of Illinois, Champaign.

Siddle-Walker, E. (1992). Falling asleep and failure among African–American students: Rethinking assumptions about process teaching. *Theory into Practice, 21,* 321–327.

Silberman, M. (1969). Behavioral expression of teachers' attitudes toward elementary school students. *Journal of Educational Psychology, 60,* 402–407.

Smith, M. (1965). Interpersonal relationships in the classroom based on the expected socio economic status of sixth-grade boys. *Teachers College Journal, 36,* 200–206.

Snow, R., Corno, L., & Jackson III, D. (1996). Individual differences in affective and conative functions (pp. 243–310). In D. Berliner & R. Calfee (Eds.), *Handbook of educational psychology.* New York: Simon & Schuster.

Tanaka, K. (1989). A response to "Are we meeting the needs of gifted Asian-students?" In C. Maker & S. Schieber (Eds.), *Defensible programs for cultural and ethnic minorities.* (Vol. II, pp. 174–178). Austin, TX: Pro-Ed.

Turner, J. C., & Meyer, D. K. (2000). Studying and understanding the instructional contexts of classrooms: Using our past to forge our future. *Educational Psychologist, 35,* 69–86.

Vygotsky, L. (1962). *Thought and language.* Cambridge, MA: MIT Press.

Weinstein, R. (1976). Reading group membership in first grade: Teacher behaviors and pupil experience over time. *Journal of Educational Psychology, 68,* 103–116.

Weinstein, R., & McKown, C. (1998). Expectancy effects in "context:" Listening to the voices of students and teachers. In J. Brophy (Ed.), *Advances in research on teaching: Expectations in the classroom* (Vol. 7, pp. 215–242). Greenwich, CT: JAI.

Weinstein, R., & Middlestadt, S. (1979). Student perceptions of teacher interactions with male high and low achievers. *Journal of Educational Psychology, 71,* 421–431.

Weinstein, R., Soule, C., Collins, F., Cone, J., Mehorn, M., & Simontacchi, K. (1991). Expectations and high school change: Teacher–researcher collaboration to prevent school failure. *American Journal of Community Psychology, 19,* 333–364.

West, C., & Anderson, T. (1976). The question of preponderant causation in teacher expectancy research. *Review of Educational Research, 46,* 185–213.

Willis, S., & Brophy, J. (1974). The origins of teachers' attitudes towards young children. *Journal of Educational Psychology, 66,* 520–529.

Wineburg, S. S. (1987). The self-fulfillment of the self-fulfilling prophecy. *Educational Researcher, 16*(9), 28–37.

Zuckerman, G. (1994). A pilot study of a 10-day course in cooperative learning or beginning Russian first graders. *Elementary School Journal, 94,* 405–420.

EDUCATIONAL PSYCHOLOGIST, *36*(2), 127–132

Increasing the Role of Educational Psychology Theory in Program Development and Evaluation

Jerome V. D'Agostino
Department of Educational Psychology
University of Arizona

Program evaluation coursework is commonly housed in educational psychology departments. Often, however, it is presented as a topic separate from learning, motivation, development, and curricular design. Some students who major in evaluation and methodology are not encouraged to take courses in these substantive areas of educational psychology, and the field of educational psychology is not presented to students as an integration of sophisticated research methods, curricular design, and the study of psychological processes that occur during learning and teaching. This article argues that evaluation has become more concerned with theory, but little work has been done in articulating, and therefore using, substantive theory to develop and evaluate social interventions. Few evaluators possess the skills and knowledge to become more involved in this area, but educational psychologists, if properly prepared in evaluation methods and substantive areas, would be in great demand to improve programs designed to address social problems.

In the broad field of educational research, program evaluation often is considered a discipline most affiliated with educational psychology. At many universities and colleges, evaluation courses commonly are offered through educational psychology departments. Many evaluators consider themselves educational psychologists, and as Baker and Niemi (1996) pointed out, the two fields have an overlapping history and share common values. Both disciplines (a) are committed to improving education, (b) consider some of the same individuals as important figures in their respective developments (such as Thorndike, Tyler, and Cronbach), (c) value sound measurement and methodology, and (d) have, at some times during their development, emphasized theory building and theory-based inquiry.

In terms of theory usage, the two fields have differed to some extent. It has always been integral to educational psychology, whereas in evaluation, the emphasis placed on theory has been given considerable and continuing attention only for about the last 20 years (Weiss, 1997a, 1997b). Further, theory in educational psychology tends to be content oriented, or substantive in nature, and primarily related to learning, motivation, development, teaching, and curriculum design. In contrast, conceptualization of theory in evaluation has been rather vague, and much less content oriented or substantive.

Theory-based, or theory-driven, evaluation represents a departure from the conventional input–output, black box evaluation. There is no one definition, approach, or method to theory-driven evaluation, but in general, the

> Root idea of theory-based evaluation is that the beliefs and assumptions underlying an intervention can be expressed in terms of a phased sequence of causes and effects (i.e., a program theory) … the evaluation is expected to collect data to see how well each step of the sequence is in fact borne out. (Weiss, 1997a, p. 501)

As Weiss (1997) pointed out, not only is the meaning of theory in evaluation unclear, it frequently is not well articulated and it is rarely used in practice. Because evaluation emphasizes research methodology, most of the discussion of theory in the field is focused on the various types of theory that are pertinent for evaluating programs. One of the more common theories that is articulated in evaluation pertains to the theory underlying the content or substance of the intervention. Although this theory type is central in many evaluation theory typologies, evaluators usually do not go into great depth when describing content theory. It is as though evaluators believe that the explicit or implicit theories that underlie programs are outside of their domain of influence. To many

Requests for reprints should be sent to Jerome D'Agostino, Department of Educational Psychology, University of Arizona, P.O. Box 210069, Tucson, AZ 85721. E-mail: jerryd@u.arizona.edu evaluators, responsibility for developing content theory is left to program designers and staff.

However, perhaps another reason evaluators do not become more involved in developing program content theory is that they are not prepared to do so, which greatly reduces their potential impact on improving social interventions. Evaluators trained solely in methodology often feel unequipped to aid in the design of programs. Frequently, evaluators are called on to examine the program long after the program has been designed and is in operation. Once programs are established, it becomes difficult to initiate changes, even in the light of evaluation evidence that reveals major limitations of the established program (Cronbach et al., 1985). Furthermore, evaluators are often unable to interpret and resolve data anomalies due to their lack of theoretical knowledge. Evaluators without an understanding of substantive theory find it difficult to develop a clear explanation of their findings, which impairs their capability to present a cogent set of recommendations for program improvement.

Educational psychologists spent considerable time designing curriculum and instructional practices based on principles of behaviorism during the late 1960s and early 1970s, but much less work has occurred more recently to develop social programs based on cognitive theories of motivation, development, and learning (Walberg & Haertel, 1992). In the area of social program development, educational psychologists historically have been underrepresented, which is unfortunate because students and scholars of educational psychology can contribute greatly to social program development and evaluation. This is especially the case given that the majority of social programs involve personnel and client learning, development, motivation, and management issues. Nonetheless, this state of affairs is beginning to change (e.g., see Stipek, de la Sota, & Weishaupt, 1999), although work in this area has considerable potential to fulfill. Developing interventions grounded in theories established in these areas is imperative to maximize the effectiveness and consistency of interventions designed to improve human conditions (Cronbach et al., 1985; Hughes, 2000). Educational psychologists can play multiple roles in program development, but it is in the area of substantive theory articulation and the transformation of theory into program activities where they are most needed.

NOTIONS OF THEORY IN THEORY-BASED EVALUATION

It is difficult to pinpoint the first person who suggested the need to consider theory in evaluation, although in his seminal work on curriculum design, Ralph W. Tyler (1949) briefly discussed the importance of theory in developing instructional objectives. In many ways, his approach to curriculum planning serves as the prototypical model of present-day program development and evaluation. Although many program designs are not based on content theory, Tyler advocated that theory plays a critical role in the development of program activities—a point that unfortunately is often overlooked. Tyler defined education as the process of changing the behavior patterns (including thinking and affect) of people, and argued that it is the responsibility of schools to determine the behaviors that are most needed by young people to fulfill their lives. The behaviors necessary for good citizenship, which young students do not possess prior to schooling, are then to be stated as actions the students can accomplish after learning, and thus, represent instructional objectives. It is the task of schools to provide students the educational experiences they need to attain the objectives, and to evaluate if students attained the objectives after instruction has occurred.

Tyler (1949) further argued that schools have to be selective in their choice of which objectives are the most important for students to attain, given that an infinite number of objectives are possible, and schools can only focus on some due to time and resource constraints. During the selection process, he contended that schools should choose objectives that are congruent with both the philosophy of education they have adopted, and the theory of learning ascribed to by the school. According to Tyler

> A theory of learning outlines the nature of the learning process, how it takes place, under what circumstances, and what sort of mechanisms operate ... since every teacher and curriculum-maker must operate on some kind of theory of learning it is useful to have this theory of learning formulated in concrete terms both to check it for its tenability and also to see its implications for the curriculum. (pp. 41–42)

Based on empirical findings, Tyler (1949) advocated theories that did not define learning as the build-up of specific stimuli and responses, but rather as the development of general modes of attack on problems and situations. Consequently, he felt that more general objectives (e.g., learning scientific principles) were more appropriate than highly specific ones. It is the school's prerogative, nonetheless, to choose a learning theory that is congruent with chosen objectives. Although he did not directly address learning theory in his explication of the role of evaluation, clearly he felt it was important for schools to study the strength of the theory and the effectiveness of the learning experiences that were to be shaped from it. Thus, Tyler was perhaps the first to discuss the importance of examining theory in evaluation.

Before theory-based evaluation became popular, others besides Tyler, such as Suchman (1967), Alkin and Fitz-Gibbon (1975), Fitz-Gibbon and Morris (1975), Rossi and Freeman (1989), and Cronbach et al. (1985) discussed the importance of theory in program design and evaluation. Many of these authors emphasized the importance of evaluating the substantive theory of programs, but few gave advice about the properties that substantive theories should possess. Most authors discussed the need to consider the underlying causes that perpetuate the problem for which the program was designed to mitigate, but descriptions of how programs were to be shaped by explications of cause–effect relations were in short supply.

Some authors focused on the various types of theory involved in program evaluation. For instance, Rossi and Freeman (1989) developed a three-pronged typology of evaluation theory. According to the authors, well-developed programs should be based on sound "impact models," which are translations of conceptual ideas into interventions founded on three fundamental hypotheses: (a) causal, (b) intervention, and (c) action. The causal hypothesis is very central. It is the set of underlying cause–effect relations that define the social problem for which an intervention is designed to address. Hence, the causal hypothesis specifies the reasons the problem persists. The intervention hypothesis explains how the program will address the causes to ameliorate the undesirable outcomes. It serves as the logic of the program, and represents what most theory-based evaluators would consider "program theory." Because the underlying cause–effect relations specified in the causal hypothesis occur naturally, however, it may not be possible to induce them with an "artificial" intervention. If certain key components of the cause are not addressed, the anticipated effects may not occur as expected. To increase the likelihood of intervention impact, Rossi and Freeman argued that an action hypothesis is necessary to describe how the program will address all key components of the cause and potential side effects that may unintentionally alter the natural flow of the cause–effect chain.

Chen (1990) expanded on Rossi and Freeman's (1989) program theory model and discussed a more extensive array of the various theories involved in evaluation. He distinguished six theory types partitioned as either normative or causative in nature. Normative theory relates to the program blueprint, or how it was designed to work. Assessing normative theory amounts to assessing if "what was done" matches "what should have been done" to realize the full potential of the program. Causative theory details how the program works. Chen stipulated three types of causative theory that provide descriptions about (a) the degree to which evaluation results generalize across implementation environments, locations, and organizational structures (generalization theory); (b) how the intervention will impact participants on anticipated and unanticipated outcomes (impact theory); and (c) how the program leads to outcomes, or of the processes that operate to cause the program consequences (intervening mechanism theory).

Weiss's (1997a) definition of theory-based evaluation is similar to Chen's (1990) intervening mechanisms theory, which both resemble Rossi and Freeman's (1989) intervention hypothesis. These notions of theory share an emphasis on the articulation of how program participants change due to experiencing intervention activities. These theories define the substance of the program, so to evaluators substantive theory clearly is very important. Ironically, however, rarely have evaluators written in great depth about various types of substantive theory, which is an area in which educational psychologists and other social science researchers can play a more vital role, given their greater focus on the factors that lead to participants' thoughts and actions. Substantive theory itself is multifaceted and dynamic, and without understanding its complexities, evaluation will not serve to improve social program delivery.

TOWARD A MORE COMPREHENSIVE UNDERSTANDING OF SUBSTANTIVE THEORY (SNOW, 1973)

Theories develop over time as empirical evidence is gathered to support or refute theoretical elements. Often theories are replaced with new ones in light of evidence that refutes all or parts of the theory. Therefore, theories function as working, testable explanations rather than stagnant end states. In his discussion of theory construction, Snow (1973) elucidated six grades of theory that represent stages in theory development. According to Snow, many, but not all, well-developed theories proceed through these six stages. He labeled each stage with a letter from A to F, with A being the most advanced level of theory development.

Formative hypotheses (F-Theory), or basic statements specifying anticipated relations between variables, represent the most rudimentary stage of theory development. Some hypotheses are formulated based on past research or experience, whereas others are based on rational thought. Many program theories can be classified at this level of theory development. Often the underlying hypotheses that form the theory are not overtly stated. In a sense, however, all programs are based, at least nominally, on a F-Theory, even if the program appears to be non-theoretical. If a program is developed to address some need, the program developers probably felt the program would be successful at reducing or eliminating the defined problem. This approach to program development, however, has led to the perpetual recycling of interventions based on faddism.

Once formative theories are developed and perhaps tested, attempts are made at reducing the variables in the hypotheses to elementary units. E-Theory (Elementisms) involves analyzing or breaking down key terms in hypotheses to reveal their internal structure. In the social sciences, where hypothesized terms are often abstract, this process is necessary if formative hypotheses are to be tested. To operationalize key terms, their key components must be identified and represented as either treatments or outcome measures. Following my argument that interventions are the tangible representations of causal terms in a theory, this step also is imperative in theory-based program design and evaluation. A major portion of program planning should involve the analysis of the key program components necessary to fully define the causes in the program theory. Programs frequently fail because some key elements of the implied or explicit formative hypothesis are missing from the intervention. Much more emphasis has been placed on the outcome end of the hypothesis. Program outcomes are often broken down into elementary program objectives. Based on Tyler's (1949) approach, it is now considered poor program planning if objectives are not specified. Commonly, however, program designers will generate lists of objectives that are not interconnected in a meaningful way to represent a theory of program participant learning or development, as Tyler had espoused.

Descriptive Theories and Taxonomies (D-Theory) comprise a level higher than elementisms because component parts are classified into an organized, conceptual system. Taxonomies of learning objectives, such as Bloom's (1956) or Gagne's (1970), are examples of D-Theory, as is Skinner's (1950) description of learning processes. Descriptive theory is rather common in theory-based evaluation, in which models are developed to describe cause–effect relations. They fall short of the next level, C-Theory, because novel constructs are not developed and rarely do these descriptive models explain why certain causes lead to certain outcomes. In this sense, most theorizing in program evaluation is not explanatory, but rather descriptive (hence, the distinction between a model and a theory).

It is rare to find classification systems in program design, but they are not uncommon in theory-based evaluation. Often evaluators find it useful to classify programs according to key dimensions to understand, for instance, how policy gets translated into practice. An evaluation of Chicago Public School reform in the mid-1990s is a good example of using classification to understand intervention implementation. Bryk, Easton, Kerbow, Rollow, and Sebring (1994) classified schools based on two separate dimensions: (a) type of local school governance (consolidated principal power, adversarial politics, maintenance politics, or strong democracy); and (b) type of organizational change (schools restoring environmental order, schools engaged in peripheral change, schools engaged in ornamental change, or schools experiencing emergent restructuring). The authors then determined the number of schools that fell within each category. This information revealed both the nature of school reform, and the extent of program success. About one third of the schools were found to be reforming as expected according to the normative theory of the reform policy.

Chen's (1990) intervening mechanisms theory also can be considered C-Theory, as long as new constructs are developed within a causal network. Often programmatic components comprise the terms in a causal network, and therefore, are at the descriptive, or D-Theory, level. At this level, program evaluation becomes an exercise in construct validation, for which multiple operational definitions of key terms are developed and compared. Although these activities would be unfeasible in many situations, the perspective would underscore that a number of different interventions can be created to operationally define the same construct. This position would move evaluation away from the study of a fixed, a priori set of program components, toward the verification of a theory of change.

The final two levels involve more theory formalization than levels C through F. Axiomatic theories, or A-Theories, are the most rigorous and entail a set of axiomatic statements and a set of theorems that can be derived as consequences of the axioms. Using rules of inference and logic, the theorems are deduced from the axioms. Often axiomatic theories are expressed as mathematical statements, such as Classical Test Theory (Allen & Yen, 1979); however, it is possible to state the theories verbally. As Snow (1973) noted, Zetterberg (1965) provided an example of a verbally-stated axiomatic theory. Zetterberg suggested that these theories can be produced by (a) listing basic concepts that are undefined except for examples, (b) defining derived concepts using the basic terms, (c) developing hypotheses from the derived concepts, and (d) classifying hypotheses as either axioms or theorems based on whether the hypotheses are independent (theorems) or derivable from the independent ones.

The relations between concepts in axiomatic theories often are presented in fine detail. In axiomatic theory, whether relations are bidirectional (if X, then Y, and if Y, then X), deterministic or probabilistic, sequential (if X, then later Y) or coextensive (if X, then also Y), sufficient (if X, then Y regardless of Z) or contingent (if X, then Y but only if Z), and necessary (if X, and only if X, then Y) or substitutable (if X, then Y, but if Z, then also Y), should be specified.

B-Theories are broken axiomatic theories that either are not supported by research findings or are clusters of axioms and statements that are not soundly connected. B-Theories representing the latter type often are hybrids of A-Theories. These theories are useful because testable hypotheses can be derived from them and they can explain some phenomena.

It is debatable, nonetheless, if program design and evaluation would benefit much from formal theory. Given that few exist in social science and that formal theories are best suited for explaining lawful phenomenon, it may be unreasonable to expect social interventions to be derived from more advanced theories. However, if educational psychology theories were incorporated into the C-Theories that underlie many programs, the result would be akin to B-Theories that would better articulate the types of programmatic activities required for program effectiveness.

THE PRESENCE OF THEORY IN TODAY'S SOCIAL PROGRAMS

Presently, nonetheless, most programs designed to improve the human condition are based on C-Theory or lower levels of theory development. Some programs consist of models that determine the specific programmatic components of the intervention. Other programs are driven by a set of objectives that may or may not be tied together in a coherent manner. Some programs contain no objectives and were developed based on the hunches of a few program developers.

For example, throughout the nation school districts are requiring students who fall behind academically to attend summer school programs. Schools are often given considerable latitude to develop curricular programs tailored to the needs of their students. Some of these summer programs probably are quite worthwhile for students. Other programs, however, probably are not very effective because they lack scope and a plan to increase student achievement. A viable action plan would include an interpretation of why certain students fall behind, perhaps in terms of their school attitudes, motivational levels, parental supports, persistent social conditions, and missed opportunities to receive quality instruction. Once this diagnosis of the problem is stated, a viable plan also would include a prognosis of how elements of the diagnosis can be addressed to mitigate the problem. Without such a plan driving the development of program activities, many summer school programs amount to "more of the same" schooling and community influences that led to the problem initially.

A number of programs today are driven by C-Theory models that specify program components. Figure 1 presents a rather typical type of program model. The Kenan model is one of the more prominent and reputable frameworks for developing family literacy interventions (Darling & Hayes, 1989). It has four components: (a) adult literacy education, which usually includes preparation for the high school equivalency test; (b) early child education; (c) parenting skills education; and (d) regular, scheduled parent–child interactions, known as PACTS.

Although the developers of the Kenan model provide program materials (which could be evaluated to determine implicit content theory), literacy programs have a great degree of latitude in how to transform the theoretical components into activities. Some would interpret this approach as ideal, because it provides individual sites the opportunity to shape the program to local needs and issues. I have found in evaluating family literacy programs that adopt the Kenan model that sites vary dramatically in their effectiveness, mainly because some sites have a well-articulated and interconnected theory of how best to serve parents and children, whereas other sites offer a disjointed and oftentimes contradictory set of program activities. As part of a formative evaluation, it would be useful for the sites to consider programmatic content questions such as

1. What pedagogical approaches are best suited to educate parents and children?
2. Is there congruence in pedagogy between the four components?
3. What is the most suitable teaching strategies to prepare staff members, and what prerequisite skills are expected of staff members given how they will be prepared?
4. Which theory of family interaction should be adopted to create viable situations for parents and children to interact together during PACT time?

This approach does not necessarily lead to a highly structured program implemented by all sites. Indeed, developers of each site should address these questions in their design or revision process.

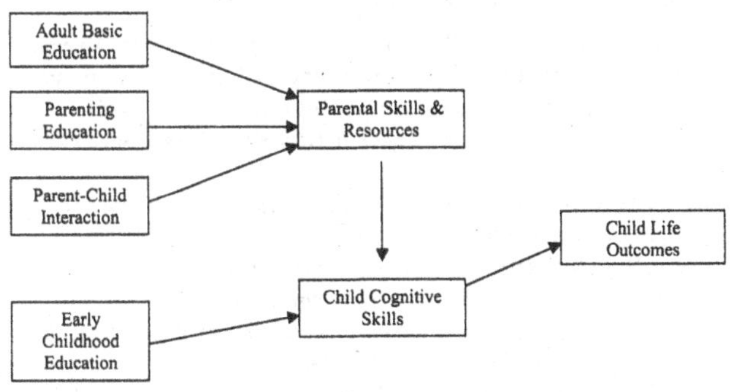

FIGURE 1 Implied causal network of the Kenan Family Literacy Model.

ADVANTAGES OF BUILDING PROGRAMS ON HIGHER ORDER THEORIES

What can be gained from striving to develop programs from B-Theories and from viewing evaluation from a scientific theory development perspective?

To address these questions, we must consider that theory development has a specific function within the scientific method. Theory development is the process of defining key concepts and explaining phenomena between these concepts. We operationalize our concepts to test the validity of our explanations, and we revise our theory in the face of conflicting empirical findings. From the scientific perspective, the program is not the theory, but rather the operationalization of key theoretical terms. From this perspective, evaluation is the testing of program theory.

Adopting a scientific approach to program development and evaluation can be beneficial for a number of reasons. First, unlike what is commonly seen in program development and evaluation, science places great emphasis and value on theory building and refinement. Indeed, crafting a good theory perhaps is more important than operationalizing testable components. All too often programs are developed based on individuals' sense of what will work, or the whims of key stakeholders and decision makers. Little planning occurs in the development of many programs, especially pertaining to the specifics of the intervention. Adopting a more scientific approach to program development would require expending more time and effort to craft the logic of the intervention.

Second, the present approach in evaluation treats interventions per se as the most central component of social programs. When programs are found to be rather ineffective, rarely are intervention components assayed to determine if the theory was properly tested. Usually, the logic underlying the theory is questioned and altered to fit the dimensions of the program. If programs were considered as testable models, they would be more prone to revision and refinement, which likely would lead to greater program effectiveness.

Third, instead of using evaluation to describe the theory, evaluation from a scientific perspective would transform into theory verification. Evaluation then would have a more dynamic role in the process of theory refinement and modification, which may lead to other interventions that are more effective than previously envisioned. Evaluation would not stop at the answer to the question, "Does the program work well?" but rather would spark other questions such as, "What needs to be done about the theory to understand the social problem much better?"

CONCLUSION

Most social programs serve one ultimate goal—to improve social conditions. Many social interventions in areas such as education, welfare, parenting, and health are designed to improve the life prospects of individuals deemed in need of skills, knowledge, or outlooks to function more effectively in the world. Consequently, social programs almost always involve the education of participants. Providing participants an intervention to get from Point A (present state) to Point B (objective) requires participants to learn new behaviors, gain new knowledge, or perceive situations differently. Interventions that work to motivate individuals to reach their potential and that are based on the consideration of how people develop are much more likely to fulfill key program objectives.

Programs also are more likely to work if thoughtful planning goes into how staff will deliver the program. To implement a program effectively, staff require certain skills and knowledge. Theories related to staff preparation, growth, "buy-in" or motivation, and selection are important in the life of a program. Oftentimes, staff develop their own theories of how the intervention works best, which may be at odds with the purported theories of the program developers. Because staff are in contact with participants to a much greater extent than many program designers, frequently staff's theories of how best to serve clients transform into more effective intervention components.

Thus, it seems logical that program evaluators would profit greatly from ascertaining both the intended and enacted substantive theories underlying social programs. Because many of these theories fall within the domain of educational psychology, knowledge of the field is extremely important in evaluating interventions designed to improve human conditions. For this reason, it is imperative that students of evaluation learn about theory development and present theories in the field. Although work in the field has been done in curricular design, few social programs have been developed with the guidance from educational psychologists. This area affords students of educational psychology the opportunity to expand their role beyond curricular design to play a part in mitigating and defining social problems.

REFERENCES

Alkin, M. C., & Fitz-Gibbon, C. T. (1975). Methods and theories of evaluating programs. *Journal of Research and Development in Education, 8*(3), 2–15.

Allen, M. J., & Yen, W. M. (1979). *Introduction to measurement theory.* Monterey, CA: Brooks/Cole.

Baker, E. L., & Niemi, D. (1996). School and program evaluation. In D. C. Berliner & R. C. Calfee (Eds.), *Handbook of educational psychology* (pp. 926–944). New York: Simon & Schuster.

Bloom, B. S. (Ed.). (1956). *Taxonomy of educational objectives: The classification of educational goals. Handbook I: Cognitive domain.* New York: Longman.

Bryk, A. S., Easton, J. Q., Kerbow, D., Rollow, S. G., & Sebring, P. A. (1994). The state of Chicago school reform. *Phi Delta Kappan, 76,* 74–78.

Chen, H. (1990). *Theory-driven evaluations.* Newbury Park, CA: Sage.

Cronbach, L., Ambron, S., Dornbusch, S., Hess, R., Hornik, R., Phillips, D., Walker, D., & Weiner, S. (1985). *Toward reform of program evaluation.* San Francisco: Jossey-Bass.

Darling, S., & Hayes, A. (1989). *Breaking the cycle of illiteracy: The Kenan Family Literacy Model Program. The William R. Kenan, Jr. Charitable Trust Family Literacy Project. Final report, 1988–1989.* Louisville, KY: National Center for Family Literacy.

Fitz-Gibbon, C. T., & Morris, L. L. (1975). Theory-based evaluation. *Evaluation Comment, 5,* 1–4.

Gagne, R. M. (1970). *The conditions of learning* (2nd ed.). New York: Holt, Rinehart & Winston.

Hughes, J. N. (2000). The essential role of theory in the science of treating children: Beyond empirically-supported treatments. *Journal of School Psychology, 38,* 301–330.

Rossi, P. H., & Freeman, H. E. (1989). *Evaluation: A systematic approach* (4th ed.). Newbury Park, CA: Sage.

Skinner, B.F. (1950). Are theories of learning necessary? *Psychological Review, 57,* 193–216.

Snow, R. E. (1973). Theory construction for research on teaching. In R. M. W. Travers (Ed.), *Second handbook of research on teaching* (pp. 77–112). Chicago: Rand McNally.

Stipek, D., de la Sota, A., & Weishaupt, L. (1999). Life lessons: An embedded classroom approach to preventing high-risk behaviors among preadolescents. *The Elementary School Journal, 99,* 433–451.

Suchman, E. (1967). *Evaluative research.* New York: Russell Sage Foundation.

Tyler, R. W. (1949). *Basic principles of curriculum and instruction.* Chicago: University of Chicago Press.

Walberg, H. J., & Haertel, G. D. (1992). Educational psychology's first century. *Journal of Educational Psychology, 84,* 6–19.

Weiss, C. H. (1997a). How can theory-based evaluation make greater headway? *Evaluation Review, 21,* 501–524.

Weiss, C. H. (1997b). Theory-based evaluation: Past, present, and future. *New Directions for Evaluation, 76,* 41–55.

Zetterberg, H. L. (1965). *On theory and verification in sociology.* Totowa, NJ: The Bedminster Press.

EDUCATIONAL PSYCHOLOGIST, *36*(2), 133–140

Educational Psychology, Social Constructivism, and Educational Practice: A Case of Emergent Identity

Mary McCaslin
Department of Educational Psychology
University of Arizona

Daniel T. Hickey
Department of Educational Psychology
University of Georgia

Psychology has long been a field beset with identity crises of one sort or another. At midcentury, psychology openly struggled with self-definition—what is psychology?—and the role—whom or what does it serve?—it was to play in individual and societal issues. Educational psychology has suffered similar identity issues. This article examines briefly the history and futility of educational psychology's in-house fights over mission and contests for theoretical dominance, allegedly in the name of unity. This article suggests instead the desirability of collaboration among diverse participants and theoretical integration for the improvement of educational practices. This article illustrates this goal with discussion of current work within a social constructivist framework.

Psychology has long been a field beset with identity crises. At midcentury, psychology openly struggled with self-definition—what is psychology?—and the role—whom or what does it serve?—it was to play in individual and societal issues. As psychologists returned from wartime placements in the military—arguably the premier era of psychology in the United States—unity was the goal. Much soul-searching and not-too-subtle persuasion over matters of vision, methods, and audience ensued. The diversity within psychology did not expedite an identity resolution, and psychology was not necessarily in total charge of that resolution. Psychology is all about what humans are and what life is about. Desired or not, psychology also becomes part of the debate on how that life should be lived. Thus, the larger culture, like psychologists themselves, also was invested in what psychology was to be and what, if any, societal limits needed to be imposed on psychological conceptions (Curti, 2000).

For example, at midcentury, in contrast to current beliefs, intelligence typically was believed inheritable and nonmodifiable. Intelligence testing and performance instrumentation were atheoretical but deemed essential in wartime personnel selection and training and the business of winning wars and world domination. In contrast, the highly theoretical yet essentially not (or not yet) empirical psychoanalytic tradition also held considerable sway, especially in the humanities and the popular culture involved in the pursuit of self and other understanding and the acceptance of personal limitations. Both ultimately made Americans—and many psychologists—uneasy (Guest, 1948), but two essential questions then are still fundamental: First, is there room for diversity, and if so, how much, in the single field of psychology? Currently the American Psychological Association has 55 divisions and even then enough psychologists felt alienated from their association identity that a new association, American Psychological Society, was formed for more academic and research-oriented psychologists.

Second, what are psychology's societal obligations? Does acceptance by the popular culture matter? Where do authentic questions and tasks originate? In the laboratory? In the legislature? In a 50-year review of *American Psychologist*, McCaslin and DiMarino-Linnen (2000) traced the evolution of these "Who are we?" "What are we for?" and "How do we know that?" questions to their more modern day instantiations. For example, the "are we scientists or practitioners" debate of the 1940s has evolved for many psychologists and citizens into the "are we biologists or pharmacists" debate in the year 2000. Psychology has found itself em-

Requests for reprints should be sent to Mary McCaslin, Department of Educational Psychology, University of Arizona, P.O. Box 210069, Tucson, AZ 85721. E-mail: mccaslin@u.arizona.edu

broiled as well in wellness initiatives and health care and pharmaceutical reform, an unexpected turn of events for many (Boneau, 1992).

AMERICAN PSYCHOLOGICAL ASSOCIATION DIVISION 15: EDUCATIONAL PSYCHOLOGY

> Division 15, Educational Psychology, provides a collegial environment for psychologists with interests in research, teaching, or practice in educational settings at all levels to present and publish papers about their work in the theory, methodology, and applications to a broad spectrum of teaching, training, and learning issues. (American Psychological Association, 2000, p. 7)

It is within this context that the field of educational psychology has developed, with its own set of identity crises and struggles with allegiance, value, and place—within psychology, education, and society (see also O'Donnell & Levin, 2001). The very place of educational psychology within the field of psychology has been questioned. Fear of second-class status—it is *applied* psychology after all—apparently has been part of being an educational psychologist for much of the 20th century. For example, most of the principles for educational practice through the 1970s were derived from research on learning and motivation that was essentially confined to animals in laboratory settings or vaguely defined college students' memorization of nonsense syllables, rather than the study of real students and teachers in schools (Melton, 1956). Worse yet, educational psychologists were accused of intentionally asking research questions that could be answered with confined animals and meaningless tasks, rather than addressing the fullness of meaningful human learning and problem solving and the role of personal value and education in its enhancement (Haggard 1954). In short, educational psychology has a history of dropping the ball, of prioritizing precision and theoretical parsimony over understanding the phenomena of learning in schools, which may not lend itself to precision and parsimony—a possibility that becomes ever more likely as we learn more about the functions of context in student learning (e.g., Turner & Meyer, 2000).

AMERICAN EDUCATIONAL RESEARCH ASSOCIATION: WHITHER EDUCATIONAL PSYCHOLOGY

Even as educational psychologists debate what it means to be a psychologist, we engage parallel debates about what it means to be in education. The American Educational Research Association (AERA) is organized around a core of twelve divisions and 140 special interest groups—none of which is explicitly "educational psychology," yet most of which can reasonably be a focus of interest for an educational psychologist. For example, AERA has distinct divisions for Learning and Instruction (Division C, formerly the unofficial home of educational psychologists), Measurement and Research Methodology (Division D), Counseling and Human Development (Division E), Social Context of Education (Division G), School Evaluation and Program Development (Division H), Teaching and Teacher Education (Division K), and Educational Policy and Politics (Division L). Educational psychologists such as us find our institutional identity increasingly expensive, and personally diffused, as multiple memberships add up fees without somehow adding up what it means to be an educational psychologist. Interestingly, where Division 15 of the American Psychological Association, Educational Psychology, offers a "Thorndike" award for scholarly excellence, AERA has a "John Dewey Society" special interest group: apparently it takes two organizations to realize our potential.

The smorgasbord approach to identity in education for educational psychologists has attenuated dissension in some areas more than others within the field. For example, "multiple methods" no longer mean three quantitative instruments and their statistical relation; rather, multiple methods now routinely encompass qualitative work with quantitative, and integration across contexts such as laboratory, micro representations, and the full context of interest. Thus, researchers observe, interview, and study learning in the university laboratory, work with individual students in the little storage rooms in schools, and observe them in their classrooms. In contrast, the infamous learning theory wars—the behaviorists versus the cognitivists—of the past century are evident still in educational psychology today, only this time around the battle is over the nature of social learning. Past learning theory wars did little to inform, let alone improve, educational practice. Educational psychology has been there and done that. It is time to move on. We return to this point.

The multiple roles that educational psychologists engage also create their own tensions. For example, to what extent can a researcher conduct a study organized around classroom learning and its participants (e.g., teachers, students, parents) and be a social policy advocate? To what extent can overlapping lenses be pure, void of conflict of interest? One solution to this conflict has been to leave it to others to interpret and implement the work. This solution sets in motion a host of problems, many in evidence in current school practices.

RESEARCH APPLICATION AND EDUCATIONAL PRACTICES

In education, the interpretation of what learning is, what is to be learned, and how that learning connects to how life is to be lived, originates in society rather than the laboratory. Business leaders, social policymakers, and citizens inform the agenda: No rats here! However, in many cases, those who conduct the research on which practices might be based also are absent. A continuing challenge for educational psychologists is the representation—at times misrepresentation and misappropriation—of educational psychology constructs by those who do not fully understand the contexts and methodological constraints within which they have been studied. Energy that might be spent proactively, in continued research or the suggested application of that research, is instead spent clarifying and restoring constructs confused by those who think they know what was studied.

In the area of classroom management, for example, Evertson, Weeks, and Randolph (1997) challenged erroneous interpretations of the management demands of complex classroom organizations. This is not a small matter as educators attempt to enlarge educational goals to include reflection, critical thinking, and problem solving rather than maintain a more restricted focus on acquisition of facts and skills. The misinterpretation of Evertson et al.'s work—to call for even more direct management and control systems in the pursuit of student reflection than those associated with a facts and skills curriculum—invites a misalignment between curricular goals and classroom management that undermines the intended instructional goal (see also Marshall, 1990; McCaslin & Good, 1992).

It is difficult to discuss misinterpretation of research; it is even more difficult to address what seems to be an over-determined dismissal or reassignment of work in educational psychology to other fields. Some educationists are like Freud in the 1930s who dismissed research verification and design experiments on his observations because they were not based on practice and case knowledge (Fancher, 2000). They simply do not believe that educational practice can be the object of research. For others, educational psychology seems best served fossilized, frozen at the turn of the 20th century, with its simple dichotomies (e.g., heredity or environment) and sweeping yet narrow visions. We prefer educational psychology at the turn of the 21st century, with all its multiple roles, messiness, and challenges—and limitations. Admittedly, there is only so much time for and utility in responding to such critics, but it does seem important that, as we consider our identity as a field, we consider as well how we let ourselves be represented by others. Especially others with whom we need to collaborate so that educational practices might be improved.

We believe that educational psychology has an important role to play in understanding and improving education for teachers and students. Misunderstandings of theoretical constructs and classroom research by teacher educators and policymakers potentially can be quite detrimental to extant practice and certainly to attempts to improve on it. It is important that, as educational psychologists, we take care in the presentation of our work and our intent for elaboration in practice, which is certainly open to challenge.

Many educational psychologists are coming relatively late, and some reluctantly, to the demands of school learning. Many educational psychologists have come to classroom practices through design experiments, in the same manner that psychologists came to psychoanalysis in the 1930s. Like their predecessors, educational psychologists are regarded by some with suspicion, with a concern that the goal of educational psychologists' interest in practice is to assert themselves as "arbiters of the mental world, able to make the final judgment of what would and would not count" (Hornstein, 1992, p. 258, cited in Fancher, 2000). Only this time it is not just what counts as "psychological knowledge"; it is also what counts as "educational practices."

CONCEPTIONS OF PRACTICE

Perhaps one avenue for better articulation of educational psychology and its potential to understand and improve practice is first to engage discussion with colleagues in psychology and in education in what is meant by "practice." Many educational psychologists are engaged in research in classrooms by way of design experiments and "applied" research to better understand what educational psychology concepts look like in practice. Others study practice to see what taxonomies and principles emerge as compared with preexisting models. Research on expectation effects is an example of the design experiment approach to practice. Laboratory research on artificially created expectation effects was applied to classrooms to see if teachers naturally formed expectations for students and, if so, if these expectations differentially organized teacher behavior and subsequent student identity (see Good & Nichols, 2001). The goal of this research, to better understand the dynamics of psychological knowledge (i.e., expectations), clarified the dynamics of the psychological construct and had apparent applications for educational practice. Importantly, the educational psychologists who engaged this research did not continue to study how inappropriate teacher expectations and related behavior might be prevented or remediated. Those applications were left to others, for example, the Teacher Expectations and Student Achievement program (see Good & Nichols, 2001, for discussion of this program). Clearly, design experiments of psychological constructs in the classroom can be valuable to educational practice as well as psychological understandings, and the field of educational psychology.

The second approach, to study practice and develop principles based on naturally occurring phenomena, is evident in the classroom management work on control of groups by Kounin (1970). Kounin was drawn to classroom observation (via videotape) precisely because prior psychological models did not account for effective teacher management of student misbehavior. Kounin transformed the question of classroom management from "how to best respond to student misbehavior" to "how to prevent student misbehavior in the first place." It is important to note that psychology and the larger culture were also invested in questions of prevention and group dynamics in the 1960s and 1970s when Kounin was conducting his research. Thus, educational practice was the source of Kounin's data, but he approached that data as a psychologist and member of the Great Society. Educational practice in classroom management has been the primary beneficiary of this work, but so too has our general understanding of the psychology of prevention and group processes.

Other conceptions of practice involve context more centrally. In this view, practice is the context within which general principles are particularized (worked out) by those who engage them for specific purposes. For example, the teaching of specific subject matters like math, science, and social studies are curricular contexts that require considerable expertise in addition to (some might argue in place of) basic concepts in educational psychology. For example, current-day teaching of inquiry-based science and small-group learning in mathematics profit from, but only so far, constructs in educational psychology. The limits of educational psychology constructs in the teaching and learning of subject matter have not always been recognized in our field. As McKeachie (APA, 2000) noted, research in these areas previously would have been seen as part of educational psychology rather than as separate areas of inquiry. It would have been assumed that a healthy exposure to Ausubel (1968), Bruner (1966), Gagné (1977), and Skinner (1974) would have been enough to understand and promote the pursuit of instructional goals and the learning of specific subject matters in the classroom. This is no longer the case. Subject matter learning is a promising area of collaboration because those who conduct research on the learning of specific disciplines likely view practice and context in ways familiar to educational psychologists. Educational psychologists also are apt to be sensitive to the psychological pressures that result when society demands teaching that is contrary to one's own knowledge and beliefs (e.g., legislated teaching of creationism).

Finally, some educators engaged in teacher and administrator education view context as the day-to-day operation of classrooms (e.g., classroom and instructional management). Prescriptions for daily operations are a more difficult arena in which to find common ground—especially if the algorithms of behaviorism are an anathema, as they appear to be for many generalist teacher educators. Knowledge of Kounin, for example, does not translate into knowledge of oneself in the face of student defiance or student failure. There is a level of prescription and a contextual embeddedness that is accessible only to the person engaged in practice at that particular time and place. It is in this arena that perhaps Freud had a point: sometimes you just have to be there to know what is going on and what to do next. Even so, we would assert that a practitioner with a tool kit based on research and constructs in educational psychology is more apt to profit from reflection on what specifically happened and what alternatives present themselves than one who does not.

In short, it seems important to recognize that "practice," and therefore the relevance of one's work to its understanding and potential improvement, is not uniformly defined among those engaged in education. The tensions between principles and skills that pervade the "relevance for practice" debate seem a promising venue for clarification of the meaning of practice and its import for integration of work across traditions. Educational psychologists, in particular, likely will profit. We are a long way from 80%-weight, laboratory-bred, naïve rats and pigeons pressing bars and pecking color keys and college sophomores avoiding eye-puffs and memorizing nonsense syllables. Yet, we suspect we still have a long way to go to understand practice and the "contexts" within which it thrives. It also seems safe to assert that the bottom line for educational psychology, no matter what the meaning of practice and context, will continue to be learning and how it is promoted and assessed. In that sense, the historic mission of educational psychology endures. We think that one promising framework, a relative newcomer to educational psychology, that may promote integration within educational psychology and with education in the pursuit of student learning, is what we term *social* or *sociohistoric* constructivism.

SOCIOHISTORIC CONSTRUCTIVISM

The sociohistoric approach is generally associated with the work of Lev S. Vygotsky and his students (e.g., Leontiev, 1974–1975; Leontiev & Luria, 1968). It has become quite influential in the past decade and numerous accounts of basic tenets and their implications for practice are available and will not be repeated here. (See, e.g., Hickey, 1997, for a discussion of sociohistoric perspectives in motivation; Hickey & McCaslin, in press, for a discussion of the potential role of sociohistoric theory in reconciling conflicts among prevailing learning and motivation theories; McCaslin & Hickey, in press, for a discussion of basic sociohistoric theory and modern elaborations related to self-regulated learning in classrooms; and Wertsch, 1985, 1991, for an historical narrative and modern directions in psychology.) Instead, we first illustrate briefly the concepts and dynamics of sociohistorical theory through the notion of "scaffolding." Second, we suggest two aspects of this approach we think important for continued consideration, particularly as they relate to practice. Our goal is to promote dialogue among educational psychologists and practitioners to better understand each other and improve practice.

Concepts and Dynamics of Sociohistoric Theory

In the sociohistoric constructivist perspective, knowledge originates in the social and physical or material worlds, thus knowledge is a

> ... cultural entity that is distributed across the physical and social environment in which that knowledge is developed and used. An individual's knowledge of a particular domain is presumed to be situated, or "stretched across" the people, books, computers, classrooms, worksheets, etc. that were present in the context in which the knowledge was learned and will continue to be used. (Hickey & McCaslin, in press, p. 18)

When knowledge is characterized in this fashion, "knowledgeable" activity is possible because the individual has become familiar with (i.e., "attuned to") the constraints and affordances that simultaneously bound and scaffold successful participation and overcome the limitations of the mind (Greeno & Goldman, 1998). As such, learning is about increasingly meaningful participation in knowledgeable sociophysical contexts. Motivation is about engagement and identity is the stuff of interpersonal relationships and opportunity. Learning, motivation, and identity are closely bound to context, specifically to participation in the activities of a community where learning is practiced and valued. Context emerges as deliberate and mutual enculturation; the social and instructional environment scaffolds the learner's participation even as the learner transforms that environment. Scaffolding suggests moveable and malleable supports that are faded when no longer needed. Essential to scaffolding is the relationship between the coparticipants. As Yowell and Smylie (1999) eloquently noted

> It is within close personal relationships marked by support of student autonomy, intersubjectivity, and intelligent sympathy that effectively scaffolded interactions between teachers and students can occur. (p. 475)

They suggested that scaffolding involves two "experts" and two "novices:" Students are the experts in their social environment. For instance, students have knowledge of the likely contingencies on their behavior that is not available to the adult novices. Adult expertise emerges when the concern is long-term consequences of actions and strategies that promote learning, motivation, and identity. Adult experts possess the future-oriented presence of mind that student novices have yet to develop.

Scaffolding is a powerful conception of teaching and learning in which teachers and students create meaningful connections between teachers' cultural knowledge and the everyday experiences and knowledge of students. Learning is not about submission to cultural authority; rather, learning renders culture yet more meaningful—for both the expert and the novice. When understood within the essential participation metaphor for learning, scaffolding embodies the essential tenets of sociohistoric constructivism (see Sfard, 1998). When understood within a more conventional acquisition metaphor for learning, scaffolding becomes just a rationale for a seemingly endless list of isolated methods.

Considering the notion of scaffolding within a participatory metaphor for learning also illustrates the integrative power of this approach: Theory development is all about the improvement of practice. In recent years there has been a significant shift in the relation between theoretical and practical work among many leading educational psychologists worldwide (see De Corte, 2000; Donovan, Pellegrino, & Bransford, 1999; National Research Council, 1999). There is increasing consensus that research embedded in the activities of practical reform will yield theoretical principles with greater scientific validity than those developed within efforts focused on sheer theory development. This new approach develops fundamental scientific understanding while designing learning environments, formulating curricula, and assessing learning. Coherence, parsimony, and predictive validity are no longer the sole questions or even the initial questions being asked of theories. Rather, the primary question of theories of learning, engagement, and instruction is whether the concepts and principles inform practice in productive ways. In practical terms, this means that critical research decisions such as the choice of independent variables will be based more on whether that choice helps refine and validate a plausible model of practice, rather than whether the variable will yield a more coherent and parsimonious theory. In such an approach, the implicit and explicit assumptions of practitioners and practices become critical, if not paramount, because these assumptions influence whether and how new models of practice will be adopted.

As the scaffolding construct illustrates, sociohistoric theory can be used as a dialectical theory, with profound implications for theory building. Greeno, Collins, and Resnick (1996) alluded to two very different ways to reconcile sociohistoric perspectives relative to other prior perspectives. One obvious approach simply assigns sociocultural activity to a higher level of aggregation, while assigning behavioral and cognitive approaches to their own, lower levels of aggregation. This approach appeals to many, perhaps because it allows broader social contexts to be characterized and studied using existing behavioral and cognitive constructs. As suggested by Greeno & Moore (1993), an alternative approach advances sociohistoric theory as a provocative tool for the dialectic reconciliation (the "synthesis") of historically opposing theories, namely the behavioral ("thesis") and cognitive ("antithesis") theories of learning and motivation. In such an approach, principles of individual behavior and principles of information processing are both understood within the same higher-order perspectives—"as special cases of more general principles of interactive function" (Greeno et al., 1996, p. 40). Thus, both the specific behaviors of individuals, in response to specific environmental stimuli, and the patterns of activity across individuals, in response to the way specific information in the environment typically is represented and transformed, are characterized as historical events. Historical events are best explained in terms of the physical and social resources that characterize the context in which those events occurred.

We argue that this "competitive" reconciliation offers a clear path out of current intractable debates over some educational practices (e.g., the impact of extrinsic reinforcers on intrinsic motivation), debates that are rooted in and emblematic of the tension between behavioral and cognitive approaches (see Hickey, 1997; Hickey & McCaslin, in press). The veracity of this expectation is being studied in research now underway that examines the consequences of increased and more public accountability standards on learning and motivation from different epistemological perspectives (Hickey, 2000).

Consider our discussion of the relationship between coparticipants in scaffolding. We noted that students could be viewed as the experts in their social environments. That expertise requires responsive contingency in the social environment—a basic tenet of behaviorism that is essential to the development of higher psychological processes in the sociohistoric perspective. The environment must be predictable to be predicted; each is essential to the development of mind. A behavioral perspective provides the ideal means for understanding and possibly addressing this critical aspect of scaffolding. In contrast, within the "levels-of-aggregation" approach to reconciliation, a behavioral characterization of this aspect of scaffolding would threaten theoretical coherence, because it would advance an orthogonal model of scaffolding that would not present the issue-of-concern in the first place. When using a sociohistoric perspective as a higher-order synthesis, however, theoretical advances around the notion of scaffolding face no such obstacles. Instead, the learners' expertise in the behavioral contingencies in their own social world is viewed as special cases of situated human activity: a particular set of constraints and affordances to which learners have become attuned.

Considerations for Research and Practice in the Sociohistoric Perspective

We conclude our discussion of sociohistoric constructivism with two suggestions for particular attention as this approach continues to develop.

Learning occurs within relationships. Scaffolding puts a very human and affectionate face on the instructional context. In the Vygotskian tradition, it merges the affective with the intellectual, what Yowell and Smylie (1999) termed *intelligent sympathy,* in recognition of the humanity of teaching and learning. Scaffolding resonates warmth and commitment. It shares features with less formal opportunities for teaching and learning that can occur between parent and child, coach and athlete, master and apprentice; relationships that often mellow with time.

Putting a human face on learning contexts challenges research and theory on classroom practice to reconceptualize constructs that often have been framed only in the physical or material worlds. For example, "allocated learning time," "competitive task structures," and "time on task" are variables that can describe quite well a behavioral approach to learning, motivation, and performance. As researchers and practitioners, we know what each means and what they are in combination. We can see that classroom. We can make predictions and have opinions about it. Scaffolding contexts are not as well served by these variables. For example, "time in scaffold" does not seem to convey much—or at least not what likely was intended. Similarly, constructs of rate and efficiency, which can readily be transferred to scaffolding instruction, nonetheless replace one theory of learning, and ability to learn, with another.

As researchers strive to better describe situative learning contexts and create taxonomies to better understand and improve them, it seems important not to overhumanize them. Imposing individual difference personality constructs on situated learning contexts is anthropomorphous, with the attendant baggage. The designation of personalized contexts shares the same difficulties that have plagued personality theory. Relative emphases within groups of individuals (or "contexts") are transformed into between-group constructs that give way to enduring and absolute labels. Labels take on a life of their own and are no longer understood as the relative constructs they are. Variations within individuals ("contexts") over time and across tasks can be lost (see Weiner, 1992).

Social beings are mammals too. The cognitive revolution moved mainstream psychology away from the body. What some may consider an overcorrection toward biology or neurology in psychology has not occurred in educational psychology, sociohistoric work included, even though Vygotsky spoke eloquently of the integration of three developing systems: biological, social, and historical. Our understanding of learning and motivation has been affected by this omission (see McCaslin & DiMarino-Linnen, 2000, for extended discussion). In psychology, cognitive variables have replaced biological and unconscious motives and their relation with learning and incentives, relations that had been fundamental constructs in the behavioral (e.g., Hull, 1951) and psychoanalytic traditions (e.g., Fromm, 1964). In education, biology most obviously is acknowledged in terms of health maintenance (e.g., school nurses), remediation of physical deprivation (e.g., students of poverty receive subsidized meals), and dysfunction (e.g., distribution of Ritalin). Our focus here is on the possible role of biology and need in motivation and learning.

McClelland (1985) persuasively argued that Atkinson's (1964) relabeling of Hull's (1951) formula—the tendency to make a response is a function of D (drive, the motive part) × H (habit, the learning part) × K (incentive in the environment part)—into three cognitive predictors of motivation seriously undermined the field's ability to predict motivated action. Something essentially human seems lost in the translation, namely the guts of it all: aroused need. This seems especially important to include in sociohistoric work. We are now in an era of student accountability that seeks to improve student test performance by raising the bar through higher standards and increasing the costs of failure by ending social promotion and diminishing the value of realized classroom achievements. High stakes testing is all about aroused motive: fear. Sociohistoric work can learn from the psychoanalytic and behavioral traditions. Classrooms are emotional places; we do well to remember that.

SMALL WINS

Educational psychologists have historically "dropped the ball" in getting smarter about work in schools (e.g., Haggard, 1954). We owe it to ourselves and to society to study things that matter to the education of students. Educational psychologists and educators must work together to anticipate issues, not merely react to those defined for us by others. This requires collaboration and communication across interrelated domains of inquiry, recognition of the legitimacy and the limits of any array of work, and appreciation of the work of the public school.

Nichols and Good (2000) documented the explosion of public interest in education in this century. As we write, the presidential race is on and those seeking office have encased themselves with school children. In contrast to previous decades (e.g., Anderson & Biddle, 1991; Berliner & Shavelson, 1988), we have policymakers' and citizens' attention. It is our time to assert our knowledge in the improvement of practice and the value of the public school. Educational policy documents that link student test scores and stock markets amid claims about the global economy have been persuasive; societal worry about global markets is fused with concern about cross-national student test performance. Student test performance has fueled criticism of the public school. Legislative remedies, like raised standards, grade retention, and summer school have created a set of problems and challenges, not all of which are in the public eye. Left-back and low-test score students assigned to summer school are members of families who experience the effects of cancelled summer plans and frightened children who are not validated in school—so they get to do it some more.

The magnitude of the task confronting educators, in one sense an exciting and challenging opportunity, reminds us of the detrimental effects of problem difficulty on problem representation, strategies for solution, and emotional dysfunction (e.g., Duncker, 1945; Weick, 1984). Weick (1984) had a point when he argued that you go for big wins only if you can tolerate high levels of arousal—otherwise, go for the "small wins." We need to anticipate and avoid flight from understanding the complexity of practice. Small wins add up, especially if we learn from each other's.

In-house battles in educational psychology for theoretical dominance ought to be a thing of the past. Similarly, the issue is not Thorndike or Dewey. The point for educational psychologists is how to integrate and reconcile these perspectives so that we can rise to the occasion of the societal spotlight on the public school. Let us transform an educational "crisis" into a fortunate opportunity—for the benefit of those who participate in the public schools and for our own emergent identity as educational psychologists who study things that matter.

REFERENCES

American Psychological Association (2000, November). An interview with Wilbert (Bill) J. McKeachie. *Newsletter for Educational Psychologists, 24,* 7–10.

American Psychological Association (2000). *Membership Dues Statement* (No. 7). Washington, DC: Author.

Anderson, D., & Biddle, B. (Eds.). (1991). *Knowledge for policy.* London: Falmer.

Atkinson, J. (1964). *An introduction to motivation.* Princeton, NJ: Van Nostrand.

Ausubel, D. P. (1968). *Educational psychology: A cognitive view.* New York: Holt, Rinehart & Winston.

Berliner, D., & Shavelson, R. (1988). Erosion of the education research infrastructure: A reply to Finn. *Educational Researcher, 17*(1), 9–12.

Boneau, A. C. (1992). Observations on psychology's past and future. *American Psychologist, 47,* 1586–1596.

Bruner, J. (1966). *Toward a theory of instruction.* Cambridge, MA: Harvard University Press.

Curti, L. (2000). *Teaching science.* Unpublished manuscript, University of Arizona, Tucson.

De Corte, E. (2000). Marrying theory building and improvement of school practice. A permanent challenge for instructional psychology. *Learning & Instruction, 10,* 249–266.

Donovan, M. S., Pellegrino, J. W., & Bransford, J. D. (Eds.). (1999). *How people learn: Bridging research to practice.* Washington, DC: National Academy Press.

Duncker, K. (1945). On problem solving. *Psychological Monographs, 58*(270), 1–113.

Evertson, C., Weeks, K., & Randolph, C. (1997, March). *Creating learning-centered classrooms: Implications for classroom management* (mimeo). Nashville, TN: Vanderbilt University.

Fancher, R. E. (2000, September). Snapshots of Freud in America, 1899–1999. *American Psychologist, 55,* 1025–1028.

Fromm, E. (1964). *The heart of man.* New York: Harper and Row.

Gagné, R. M. (1977). *The conditions of learning* (3rd ed.). New York: Holt, Rinehart & Winston.

Good, T., & Nichols, S. (2001). Expectancy effects in the classroom: A special focus on improving the reading performance of minority students in first grade classrooms. *Educational Psychologist, 36,* 113–126.

Greeno, J. G., Collins, A. M., & Resnick, L. (1996). Cognition and learning. In D. Berliner & R. Calfee (Eds.), *Handbook of educational psychology* (pp. 15–46). New York: Macmillan.

Greeno, J. G., & Goldman, S. V. (1998). Thinking practices. Images of thinking and learning in education. In J. G. Greeno and S. Goldman (Eds.), *Thinking practices in mathematics and science learning* (pp. 1–16). Mahwah, NJ: Lawrence Erlbaum Associates, Inc.

Greeno, J. G., & Moore, J. L. (1993). Situativity and symbols: A response to Vera and Simon. *Cognitive Science, 17,* 49–60.

Guest, L. (1948). The public's attitudes toward psychologists. *American Psychologist, 3,* 135–139.

Haggard, E. (1954). The proper concern of educational psychologists. *American Psychologist, 9,* 539–543.

Hickey, D. (1997). Motivation and contemporary socio-constructivist instructional perspectives. *Educational Psychologist, 32,* 175–193.

Hickey, D. T. (2000). *Assessment, motivation, & epistemological reconciliation in a technology-supported learning environment* (Grant REC–9909732). The National Science Foundation, Division on Research, Evaluation, & Communication to the University of Georgia.

Hickey, D. T., & McCaslin, M. (in press). A comparative, sociocultural analysis of context and motivation. In S. Volet and S. Järvelä (Eds.), *Motivation in learning contexts: Theoretical and Methodological implications.* Oxford: Pergamon.

Hull, C. (1951). *Essentials of behavior.* New Haven, CT: Yale University Press.

Kounin, J. (1970). *Discipline and group management in classrooms.* New York: Holt, Rinehart & Winston.

Leontiev, A. N. (1974–1975). The problem of activity in Soviet psychology. *Soviet Psychology, 13,* 4–33.

Leontiev, A. N., & Luria, A, R. (1968). The psychological ideas of L. S. Vygotsky. In B. B. Wolman (Ed.), *Historical roots of contemporary psychology* (pp. 338–367). New York: Harper & Row.

Marshall, H. (1990). Beyond the workplace metaphor: Toward conceptualizing the classroom as a learning setting. *Theory into Practice, 29,* 94–101.

McCaslin, M., & DiMarino-Linnen, E. (2000). Motivation and learning in school: Societal contexts, psychological constructs, and educational practices. In T. Good (Ed.), *American education: Yesterday, today, and tomorrow,* (Part II, pp. 84–151). Chicago: University of Chicago Press.

McCaslin, M., & Good, T. (1992). Compliant cognition: The misalliance of management and instructional goals in current school reform. *Educational Researcher, 21*(3), 4–17.

McCaslin, M., & Hickey, D. T. (in press). Self-regulated learning and academic achievement: A Vygotskian view. In B. Zimmerman and D. Schunk (Eds.), *Self-regulated learning and academic achievement: Theory, research, and practice* (2nd ed., pp. 227–252). Mahwah, NJ: Lawrence Erlbaum Associates, Inc.

McClelland, D. (1985). How motives, skills, and values determine what people do. *American Psychologist, 40,* 812–825.

Melton, A. (1956). Present accomplishment and future trends in problem-solving and learning theory. *American Psychologist, 11,* 278–281.

National Research Council (1999). *Improving student learning: A strategic plan for education research and its utilization* (Committee on a Feasibility Study for a Strategic Education Research Program). Washington, DC: National Academy Press.

Nichols, S. L., & Good, T. L. (2000). Education and society, 1900–2000: Selected snapshots of then and now. In T. Good (Ed.), *American education: Yesterday, today, and tomorrow* (Part 2, pp. 1–52). Chicago: University of Chicago Press.

O'Donnell, A. M., & Levin, J. R. (2001). Educational psychology's healthy growing pains. *Educational Psychologist, 36,* 73–82.

Sfard, A. (1998). On the two metaphors for learning and the danger of choosing just one. *Educational Researcher, 27*(2), 4–13.

Skinner, B. F. (1974). *About behaviorism.* New York: Knopf.

Turner, J., & Meyer D. (2000). Studying and understanding the instructional contexts of classrooms: Using our past to forge our future. *Educational Psychologist, 32,* 69–85.

Weick, K. E. (1984). Small wins: Redefining the scale of social problems. *American Psychologist, 39,* 40–49.

Weiner, B. (1992). *Human motivation: Metaphors, theories, and research.* London: Sage.

Wertsch, J. (Ed.). (1985). *Culture, communication, and cognition: Vygotskian perspectives.* New York: Cambridge University Press.

Wertsch, J. V. (1991). *Voices of the mind: A socio-cultural approach to mediated action.* Cambridge, MA: Harvard University Press.

Yowell, C. M., & Smylie, M. A. (1999). Self-regulation in democratic communities. *Elementary School Journal, 99,* 469–490.